EDITED BY
NIGEL CLARK
and
BILL PRICE

tall buildings

A STRATEGIC DESIGN GUIDE

2nd edition

RIBA ✶ Publishing

British Council for Offices

Council on Tall Buildings and Urban Habitat

© British Council of Offices (BCO), 2016
First edition published 2005

Published by RIBA Publishing, part of RIBA Enterprises Ltd,
The Old Post Office, St Nicholas Street, Newcastle upon Tyne, NE1 1RH

ISBN 978 1 85946 618 6
978 1 85946 723 7 (Ebook)

British Library Cataloguing-in-Publication Data
A catalogue record for this book is available from the British Library.

Commissioning Editor: Fay Gibbons
Production: Kate Mackillop
Typeset and designed by Paul Tilby
Printed and bound by Page Bros Ltd, Norwich

www.ribaenterprises.com

1007678769

British Council for Offices (BCO)

The British Council for Offices is the UK's leading member organisation representing the interests of all those who occupy, design, build, own or manage offices in the UK. Since its inception in 1990, the BCO has become the leading forum for the discussion and debate of issues affecting the office sector, providing thought leadership in all issues related to the creation and use of office space. From communicating best practice through the BCO's Guide to Specification, to analysing industry issues such as the recent office-to-residential conversion legislation, the BCO aims to stimulate new thinking on the design, development and occupation of offices across the UK. Alongside an extensive research programme, the BCO runs its annual awards, conference and regular events to recognise the most innovative workplaces in the UK and to bring together the people behind them.

The BCO welcomes this publication as it recognises that offices don't just house companies, they hold people, and so what goes on inside them is paramount to workplace wellbeing.

Council on Tall Buildings and Urban Habitat (CTBUH)

The Council on Tall Buildings and Urban Habitat is the world's leading resource for professionals focused on the inception, design, construction and operation of tall buildings and future cities. Founded in 1969 and headquartered at Chicago's historic Monroe Building, the CTBUH is a not-for-profit organisation with an Asia Headquarters office at Tongji University, Shanghai; a Research Office at Iuav University, Venice, Italy; and a Chicago Research and Academic Office at the Illinois Institute of Technology. CTBUH facilitates the exchange of the latest knowledge available on tall buildings around the world through publications, research, events, working groups, web resources and its extensive network of international representatives. The Council's research department is spearheading the investigation of the next generation of tall buildings by aiding original research on sustainability and key development issues. The Council's free database on tall buildings, The Skyscraper Center, is updated daily with detailed information, images, data and news. The CTBUH also developed the international standards for measuring tall building height and is recognised as the arbiter for bestowing such designations as 'The World's Tallest Building'.

About the Editors

Nigel Clark

Nigel Clark is Technical Director with Hilson Moran and has been involved in the design and construction of buildings for over 38 years. Having graduated from the London South Bank University in 1979, his career started in the public sector, where he was involved in the design of large-scale educational, leisure, residential and court buildings. He joined Hilson Moran in 1988 where he was involved in delivering a number of tall buildings at Canary Wharf, 30 St Mary Axe (SwissRe – also known as The Gherkin) and more recently 20 Fenchurch Street in London. He is currently involved in a number of large commercial, mixed use and regeneration schemes totalling over 600,000 sqm, including 1 Bank Street at Canary Wharf and 100 Bishopsgate in the City of London. In particular, Nigel has considerable experience in the application of advanced software to inform the design process, the application of low and zero carbon and renewable technologies, the energy performance of buildings, as well as façade design solutions to ensure optimum comfort and building performance. He is also an advocate in the potential for BIM to revolutionise the way buildings are designed, constructed and managed. He regularly provides advice on all aspects of the design of buildings in the UK, Europe and the Middle East with an emphasis on tall buildings and environmentally progressive buildings. Nigel has been London Chairman of the Judges for the BCO Awards and has also been a contributor to the recent BCO Guides to Specification and Fit Out.

Bill Price

Bill Price is a director at WSP | Parsons Brinckerhoff and a structural engineer by background. He worked on the multi-award winning Shard from the earliest stages of design development alongside Sellar Property Group, London Borough of Southwark, Renzo Piano Building Workshop, Network Rail and the other designers and stakeholders. In addition, Bill is working on exciting commercial initiatives for Network Rail and Transport for London, a large mixed-use station regeneration project, a major new stadium and new cultural facilities in London and Stratford.

Bill has spoken at numerous conferences and events on the subject of high-rise, sustainability, transportation infrastructure and engineering design. In addition, Bill has travelled extensively in connection with project opportunities in the US, Canada, Europe, Russia, Middle East and North Africa.

Bill has strong links to the BCO and is a supporter of the organisation's activity and contribution to the industry. He has attended its annual conference for over 15 years and has organised its technical building visits in New York, Madrid and, most recently, Chicago.

Acknowledgements

Our sincere thanks go to all the professionals who have contributed to this publication by providing their expertise and guidance for the benefit of others who are either intrigued by, or involved in, the construction and delivery of tall buildings. It was a concerted desire to bring together a larger number of contributors than the first edition to give as balanced, wide ranging and, hopefully, interesting publication as possible. Such a large list of contributors brought its challenges but we hope the efforts have resulted in a second edition in which everyone will find something of interest and expand their understanding of what makes tall buildings great.

A special acknowledgement must also go to the British Council of Offices and the Council on Tall Buildings and Urban Habitat for their continued support and for commissioning this second edition of *Tall Buildings – A Strategic Design Guide*. A particular acknowledgement must also go to Braden Wyatt for his assistance, support and persistence in collating the various images and obtaining the permissions for their use. His help during the editing of this publication has been invaluable.

To all the contributors for their efforts and willingness to share their expertise so freely and generously and to everyone else who has given permission for material to be included, thank you.

Nigel Clark and Bill Price

About the Contributors

NIGEL BIDWELL

Nigel is a Partner and Architect at Farrells. He is involved in a number of London's high-profile developments at Convoys Wharf, Earls Court and Old Oak Common, and has significant experience in the integration of tall buildings within new regenerative schemes. In addition, he is a member of a number of Design Review panels and comments regularly on tall building proposals emerging in the capital.

MEIKE BORCHERS

Meike is an Associate Director at WSP|Parsons Brinckerhoff and has 15 years of experience in structural design and sustainability in the built environment. She has worked on a number of high-profile projects, such as MASDAR and 40 Leadenhall Street. Her expertise is in environmental performance analysis and lifecycle assessments, energy-efficient technologies, climate change adaptation of buildings and sustainable materials.

STEVE BOSI

A chartered structural engineer by profession, Steve has been working in façade engineering consultancy for over 25 years. Steve leads the UK Façade Engineering business as well as forming part of the global WSP | Parsons Brinckerhoff resource base which now consists of almost 100 façade engineers globally. During this time he has gained significant experience in the design and construction of building envelopes for a variety of buildings with signature architects and blue chip clients.

DAVID BOWNASS

David has over 35 years' experience in energy infrastructure and the built environment. His early career was spent in building services engineering, moving into managing large multi-discipline engineering projects and development master planning. He currently manages the WSP|Parsons Brinckerhoff Sustainable Buildings Group (SBG). His broader business role involves providing strategic sustainability leadership and enhancing

their sustainability profile in the external market. His understanding of the current and future energy and sustainability agenda, particularly in the UK market, is highly valued.

JOSEPH BURNS

Joseph joined Thornton Tomasetti in 1995 and has more than 30 years' experience designing structures as well as investigating and renovating existing buildings. His credits span a wide spectrum of building types and market sectors. A member of Thornton Tomasetti's board of directors, he is the Managing Principal overseeing the firm's emerging practice areas and operations in Europe, the Middle East, India and Brazil.

ALAN CRONIN

Alan is a Divisional Director at Hilson Moran, jointly responsible for the Vertical Transportation group. Alan has been responsible for the design of many large commercial, residential and mixed-use developments with a particular emphasis on high-rise buildings in the UK, Europe and the UAE, including 20 Fenchurch Street and the 312m-tall Landmark Tower in Abu Dhabi. He is a member of the CTBUH and the CIBSE Lift groups.

CHRIS DRIVER-WILLIAMS

As WSP| Parsons Brinckerhoff UK's Head of Security Consulting, Chris brings with him 25 years of military and commercial experience in counter-terrorism, national infrastructure protection, blast and explosives engineering, and security and risk management. A former UK special forces bomb disposal operator and recipient of the Queen's Gallantry Medal, he is also a Freeman of the City of London, a Fellow of the Institute of Explosive Engineers, and a Member of the Chartered Management Institute and the International Association of Bomb Technicians and Investigators (IABTI).

GREG DUNN

Greg is a Principal with Adamson Associates, an architectural firm widely known for its role as Executive Architect. Greg has been involved for many years in major London high-rise developments, including several of the towers at Canary Wharf and The Shard at London Bridge. His international experience also includes completed towers in Milan, New York and Shanghai. He has spoken internationally at tall building conferences on trends in high-rise development.

DAVID ELDER

David Elder is a Director with Mace and is Head of Planning and Preconstruction, leading a team of over 100 staff across nine business sectors. He was the Operations Director leading the planning and logistics function at London Bridge Quarter, which included The Shard – Europe's tallest building – and has given advice to clients around the world on the construction of tall buildings.

YAIR GINOR

Yair is an Equity Partner and Director of Lipton Rogers Developments, responsible for originating and overseeing the delivery of large-scale development projects, including 22 Bishopsgate. He has led developments totalling over £1.5bn value, including Elizabeth House, Waterloo and the mixed-use regeneration of Hawley Wharf, Camden. Yair holds an MPhil in Real Estate Finance from the University of Cambridge and a BArch in Architecture. He is a visiting lecturer in the Said Business School, University of Oxford, as well as the department of Land Economy, University of Cambridge.

JOHN HANNAH

John is the Estimating Director for Brookfield Multiplex Construction Europe and oversees the estimating for all major UK projects, predominantly in London, for a business with a turnover of £1bn. He has worked in the construction industry for over 20 years in both the public and private sectors. In addition, John has studied at

Glasgow Caledonian University, obtaining degrees in Construction Management and Construction Economics. Recently he completed an MSt in Construction Engineering at the University of Cambridge.

ROSS HARVEY

Ross is a Technical Director for WSP | Parsons Brinckerhoff. He has been involved in a number of high-profile buildings throughout his career; he is passionate about the design and successful delivery of complex projects. He is currently involved in 22 Bishopsgate and Principal Tower developments.

DAVID HODGE

David is Head of Mechanical and Electrical Engineering and Sustainability at Canary Wharf Contractors Limited. He is responsible for ensuring that the group's buildings achieve the highest levels of energy efficiency and sustainability. Notable recent projects include 20 Fenchurch Street, which achieved an Excellent 2011 BREEAM rating with a score of 80.2%, and the refurbishment of One Canada Square, which included significant energy-efficiency enhancements.

JONATHAN INMAN

Jonathan is a Director and Civil Engineer at Skanska UK. He led the engineering teams in the construction of the award-winning 30 St Mary Axe (The Gherkin) and Heron Tower buildings. He collaborates on projects in London, Europe and North America. In addition, he promotes Skanska UK engineering innovation and development activities.

GARETH LEWIS

Gareth is a Mace Group Board Director, with more than 25 years' experience in the construction industry. He specialises in running complex major projects in London. Some of Gareth's most high-profile projects include Heathrow Terminal 5 and The Shard and London Bridge Quarter. Gareth was appointed Chief Operating Officer of Mace's construction business in the UK in 2007.

JENNY MAC DONNELL

Jenny is a Director at the British Council for Offices where she leads the research and policy programme. Notable projects include the publication of the BCO Guide to Specification for Offices, which sets the standards for office development across the UK. She works closely with a wide range of professionals in the office sector, including the BCO's Occupier Group and the BCO Banking Peer Review Group.

FRANK MCLEOD

Frank is the UK Head of Project Technology and is responsible for the development and implementation of a design delivery philosophy, 'Drive for Change', at WSP|Parsons Brinckerhoff. He is a Chartered Structural Engineer and has worked in the professional services for over 30 years. Frank worked with BAA plc during the preparation of Rethinking Construction, which developed a clear vision of how manufacturing and product-based ideals could be blended into the construction industry.

KAMRAN MOAZAMI

Kamran has over 34 years of structural engineering experience in the USA, Middle East, China and the United Kingdom. He is head of WSP | Parsons Brinckerhoff UK structural engineering discipline. Kamran has been responsible for the concept design of several award-winning projects in the UK and USA, including The Shard, named 'Project of the Year' at the ENR 2013 Awards.

PETER MURRAY

Peter is Chairman of the New London Architecture centre, which first revealed that some 263 tall buildings are currently in the pipeline in London. He is author of *The Saga of Sydney Opera House* – the story of the first modern global icon – and is about to publish a book on the Leadenhall Building designed by Rogers Stirk Harbour + Partners, winner of the City of London Building of the Year 2015 and an important icon in the Square Mile.

MAT OAKLEY

Mat is Head of Savills UK and European commercial property research team. His experience includes work on a variety of topics including inward investment into various office markets, the impact of major infrastructure developments, economic impact analyses, and assessing demand for and master planning major mixed-use developments. He is a regular conference speaker on all aspects of the UK and European commercial property markets, and sits on the board of the BCO.

MARK O'CONNOR

Mark is a Director and Head of Analysis & Design in WSP | Parsons Brinckerhoff UK structures business. He is responsible for the conceptual and schematic designs of the lateral stability systems of tall buildings. He is also responsible for technical review of all tall building designs in the UK's extensive portfolio of projects. Notable projects include The Shard, Principal Place and 22 Bishopsgate.

ERIC PARRY

Eric established Eric Parry Architects in 1983. Under his leadership, the practice has developed a reputation for delivering beautifully crafted and well-considered buildings that respond to their context. London has been the focus and the setting for most of his work. He was elected Royal Academician (RA) in 2006 and awarded the honorary degree of Doctor of Arts from the University of Bath in 2012.

JAMES PELLATT

James is Head of Projects at Great Portland Estates and leads the delivery of their wide and varied development portfolio. He has planned and developed tall buildings at 100 Bishopsgate, 240 Blackfriars and continues to seek opportunities for towers where appropriate in Central London. Great Portland Estates were the first major developer to implement the use of BIM from a client mandate in Central London at 240 Blackfriars.

LUKASZ PLATKOWSKI

Lukasz is a Principal at Gensler and is their Tall Buildings Practice Area Leader and Regional Design Leader for the EMEA region. Since joining Gensler in 1999, Lukasz has become known for his passion, talent and innovation in design. He leads a number of projects in the UK, Europe and Middle East that are changing industry standards and redefining 'world-class' design. He contributes to BCO CTBUH Strategic Guidelines and sits on numerous jury panels, including *World Architectural News* Commercial Office Awards and LEAF Awards.

COLIN ROBERTS

Colin is a Principal Fire Consultant at Hilson Moran in London. He has contributed to the fire safety design of tall buildings in London, Hong Kong and Sydney. Notable projects include The Shard at over 300m and the 140m-high No 1 Bligh Street in Sydney. He specialises in strategies that permit flexibility in the use of atrium within tall buildings.

DAVID SCOTT

David is the Lead Structural Director with the Laing O'Rourke Engineering Excellence Team where he works with a team of engineers and scientists in the continuous pursuit of innovation and engineering, on a wide range of building, infrastructure and research projects. David is Past-Chairman of the CTBUH and has designed many tall buildings around the world. In 2010 he was elected as a fellow of the Royal Society of Edinburgh and in 2014 he was elected to the Royal Academy of Engineering.

PAUL SCOTT

Paul was a Partner at Make and spent over 20 years shaping cities around the world on schemes ranging from boutique to iconic. Paul was leading several high-profile projects, including 40 Leadenhall Street in London's insurance district; Wynyard Place, an office, station concourse and retail development in Sydney; and two striking residential towers in Mumbai. Paul championed the role tall buildings play in supporting population growth while mitigating their impact on global warming to create more integrated and sustainable spaces. Tragically, Paul passed away in January 2016.

DARIO TRABUCCO

Dario is the Research Manager at the Council on Tall Buildings and Urban Habitat and a tenured researcher at the Iuav University of Venice, Italy. He has been involved in numerous research projects on tall buildings, investigating various aspect of tall building technology and lifecycle sustainability.

STEVE WATTS

Steve is a cost consultant with over 25 years' experience and unrivalled knowledge of the economics of tall buildings. A founding Partner of alinea Consulting LLP, he previously headed the global Tall Buildings Group at Davis Langdon (then AECOM). Steve has worked on many prominent UK and international towers, including the HSBC tower, The Shard and 22 Bishopsgate. He has contributed to several High-Rise Cost Models and the CTBUH's *Tall Buildings Reference Book*, and is also Treasurer and Trustee of the CTBUH and Chair of its UK Chapter.

COLIN WILSON

Colin Wilson is a planner and urban designer who has worked in London for the last 24 years. He currently manages the Greater London Authority's Development and Projects Team and is responsible for dealing with the referred strategic planning applications, Mayoral call-ins and the production of the Mayor's Opportunity Area Planning Frameworks, including the Vauxhall Nine Elms and White City Planning Frameworks. He has also contributed to the London Plan tall building and design policies and the development of the London View Management Framework.

DR ANTONY WOOD

Antony has been Executive Director of the CTBUH since 2006. Based at the Illinois Institute of Technology, he is a Research Professor in the College of Architecture and also a Visiting Professor of Tall Buildings at the College of Architecture and Urban Planning at Tongji University, Shanghai. His field of specialism is the design – particularly the sustainable design – of tall buildings. Prior to his tenure with CTBUH, Antony worked as an architect in Hong Kong, Bangkok, Kuala Lumpur, Jakarta and London.

Contents

Preface

In 2005, the British Council for Offices (BCO) published the first edition of *Tall Buildings: A Strategic Design Guide*. Since then there have been significant changes in the world of tall buildings, particularly in the London skyline. Some of the buildings that were in the planning stages in 2005 are now complete, and many more are in both early and advanced stages of development. With this in mind, the time seemed right to produce an update.

In this second edition, the BCO have joined with the Council on Tall Buildings and Urban Habitat (CTBUH) in order to broaden the geographical scope from a predominantly UK focus, to one of international remit. We feel this approach better reflects the reality of the tall building scene today, where many of the tallest and most iconic skyscrapers are located throughout the world's continents.

There are a number of additions and improvements to this edition of *Tall Buildings*. Thought pieces by key industry experts open the book with some intriguing insights into where we are today and where we should be focussing our attention in the future with regard to the vertical urban landscape. The addition of interviews to Chapter 2, *Occupier Perspectives*, also provides an interesting, first-hand account of why organisations choose to occupy tall buildings in the first place.

A decision was made to expand and break up the chapters on design aims and development, to reflect better the wide range of specialists and expertise needed to deliver tall buildings – from design and engineering to construction and management. As part of this change, a brand-new chapter on BIM brings the book up to date with modern practice and technology. This fills an important gap in the book's treatment of design strategy, as the success of tall buildings relies heavily on a high degree of coordination and efficient information exchange.

Chapter 9, *End Of Life Of A Tall Building*, expands on an increasingly important topic, the sustainability agenda, amid efforts to move toward circular economy principles and long-term planning to protect skylines and resources for future generations. Finally, in this edition we decided to end by looking to the future, with Chapter 10, *The Next Generation*, considering the likely drivers of continued development and guidelines for the next generation of tall buildings.

As with the previous edition, this publication is not an in-depth guide to producing tall buildings, but rather a 'road map' of key aspects to consider in their generation and evaluation. It has been produced by professionals with specialist knowledge in the fields covered and we are very grateful to the editors, Nigel Clark and Bill Price, for sharing their professional expertise, skills and, most particularly, their time with us. We are also grateful to the large number of contributors who shared their own valuable knowledge and experience under the leadership of Nigel and Bill.

We hope this second edition will contribute in some small way towards the creation of even better tall buildings for future generations to use and, more importantly, enjoy.

Richard Kauntze
British Council for Offices

Dr Antony Wood
Council on Tall Buildings and Urban Habitat

Introduction

The BCO first published a tall buildings design guide in 2005. At that time the London skyline was starting to change significantly after a period of relative stability since the 1970s. A number of tall buildings were also in the early stages of design and planning process. The 2005 guide showcased many of the proposals for London and discussed particular attributes of these buildings, together with the effects they would have on the City of London, the occupiers and the public.

In the period since 2005 many of the showcased buildings have been constructed and the skyline of London changed further. There has also been time for many additional tall buildings (mostly residential) to be planned and constructed. The worst UK recession since the 1930s commenced in 2008 and, at a global level, more people were living in cities than in traditional rural locations.

With the continuing demand for tall buildings and the appetite for change London has embraced, the BCO felt that the 2005 guide needed refreshing and updating. This second edition of the guide covers a wider range of content than the first edition and is comprehensively revised.

To set the scene, it is useful to understand five emerging trends and these are set out below. As a precursor, however, it is worth discussing what constitutes 'tall'. It has been suggested that 'tallness' could be about height relative to context, or perhaps proportion. In this book the word 'slender' appears and that is essentially about proportion. We are concerned here with modern cities and buildings, so context and relative scale becomes secondary.

In New York, tall is frequently considered to be 50 storeys and for an office this could be 200m. In the UK, 30 storeys, or around 100m, is more likely to attract that title. Two other titles have appeared in recent times, including 'supertall' for a building over 300m and 'megatall' for over 600m. All these kinds of tall buildings are mentioned in the book and as of April 2016 there were 101 supertall and three megatall buildings completed and occupied globally.

← *The Shard, London*

Contributors

Nigel Clark
Bill Price
Dr Antony Wood

Recent Trends

Figure 0.1:
Current tallest 20 buildings in the world (data as of April 2016)

As more of the world becomes 'modern', the building boom that began in the late 1990s and early 2000s has expanded across virtually the entire globe. Even as a global recession hit in 2008–09, countries just emerging into their economic prime continued to build. To demonstrate this, Figure 0.1 shows the current tallest 20 buildings in the world, their heights and locations. Now, it seems that almost all cities globally have been developing their urban habitat skyward. This boom can be described in terms of five emergent trends.

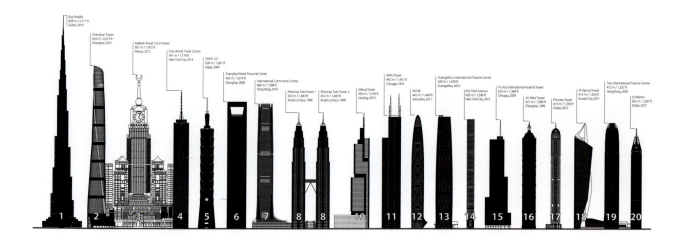

Trend 1: More tall buildings

Research by the CTBUH illustrates the recent explosive growth of tall buildings by plotting the number of skyscrapers 200m or higher completed each year since 1960 (see Figure 0.2). This shows the steady build up during the 1990s, followed by the exponential growth from the mid-2000s onwards. Interestingly, although there has been a very definite drop in skyscraper activity in most Western countries, this is expected to be offset by activity in Asia generally – and China specifically – such that we expect the global number of tall buildings completed each year to keep climbing for the foreseeable future. In 2015, for instance, an all-time record 106 buildings of 200m or higher were completed.

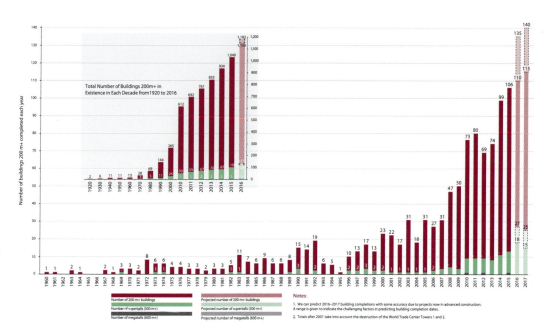

Figure 0.2:
Total number and annual completion of buildings over 200m and 300m (data as of January 2016)

The detailed statistics are quite staggering. Some 72 of the current 100 tallest buildings in the world have been completed since the end of 2005, with 13 of these buildings completed in 2015 alone.

Trend 2: Taller tall buildings

Tall buildings are indisputably getting taller, both in individual achievement and in collective average height. As Figure 0.3 shows, the average height of the world's 100 tallest buildings has increased over 200m (132%) since 1930, with 65m growth (25.3%) in the period 2000–16 alone. At the 'world's tallest' end of the scale, the year 2010 witnessed an incredible feat with the completion of the 828m-tall Burj Khalifa in Dubai.

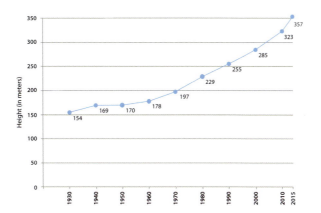

← *Figure 0.3:*
Average height of the 100 tallest buildings each decade, from 1930–2015 (data as of January 2016)

At no previous time in the history of the 'world's tallest' (see Figure 0.4) has any building surpassed its predecessor by more than 68m (221ft), but Burj Khalifa achieved an unprecedented 320m (1,050ft) leap over the previous world's tallest, TAIPEI 101. The total height of the Burj Khalifa is just 5m shy of the equivalent height of putting the Empire State Building on top of Petronas Towers (both former 'world's tallest' buildings).

Continuing this trajectory, the world's next tallest – expected to be the Jeddah Tower in Jeddah, Saudi Arabia – will be over 1,000m in height. Though the recent 'world's tallest' achievements tend to skew all impression of tall building height, the reality is that the completion of a supertall building over 300m high is still a significant urban and technological achievement.

↓ *Figure 0.4:*
History of the 'world's tallest building' (data as of January 2016)

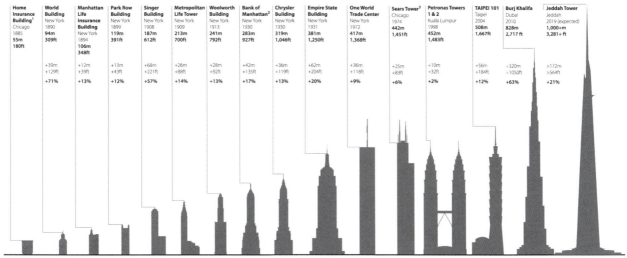

[1] While the Home Insurance Building was never the tallest building in the world, it is considered the first skyscraper constructed (framed/non-loadbearing façade construction) and thus the first "tall building" as defined by the CTBUH.

[2] Now known as The Trump Building, "Bank of Manhattan" was the building's title when it was the "World's Tallest Building."

[3] Now known as Willis Tower, "Sears Tower" was the building's title when it was the "World's Tallest Building."

Trend 3: Changing locations

The predominant location of the tallest buildings in the world has been changing rapidly (see Figure 0.5). As recently as 1990, 80% of the '100 world's tallest' were located in North America, now that figure is only 17%, with the shift occurring predominantly to Asia (48%) and the Middle East (28%).

→ *Figure 0.5:*
100 tallest buildings by location each decade, from 1930–2015 (data as of January 2016)

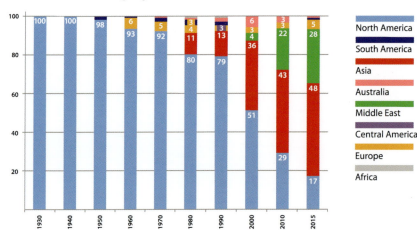

100 tallest buildings by location

Trend 4: Changing functions

There has also been a major move away from the predominantly office function which dominated the 'tallest' lists for many decades (see Figure 0.6). While 85% of the '100 world's tallest' buildings were office buildings as recently as 2000, that number has shrunk to 38% in 2015. Over the same period, mixed-use functions grew from 12% to 41%.

The rapid urbanisation of developing countries partially explains why many of these buildings are now residential in nature rather than commercial. As these countries urbanise, new housing is being constructed at a rapid pace. There are other reasons for this shift, however, especially towards mixed-use, which is considered as a hedge against fluctuating demand for office, residential and hotel functions by including them all in the building programme. It also makes sense that if great height is the main objective of the project, then it is easier to achieve this with a residential rather than an office function.

→ *Figure 0.6:*
100 tallest buildings by function each decade, from 1930–2015 (data as of January 2016)

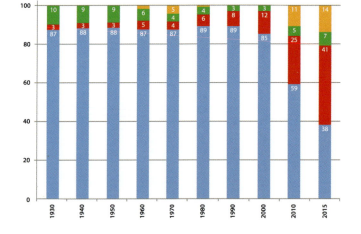

100 tallest buildings by function

Trend 5: Changing materials

The change in structural material has also been very significant over the past few decades. All steel-structure buildings have dropped to just 11% from 89% in 1970 in favour of concrete or composite structures (see Figure 0.7).

The reasons for the trend towards concrete/composite structure in the world's tallest buildings are multi-layered. It is partly a product of the developing countries where these projects are located, which are much more likely to have concrete expertise than steel. Cost is also a significant factor, with concrete being less costly than steel. The aforementioned change towards residential and mixed-use functions is also influential, since the fire, acoustic and cellular requirements of residential construction lend themselves better to concrete construction rather than open-plan-enabling steel. There are also many who believe that the increased performance required of the structure at great height – through the required damping of movement (especially in residential towers, whose occupants are especially sensitive to movements) as well as the transfer of vertical loads – can be more adequately handled by steel and concrete acting together compositely, rather than by one material alone.

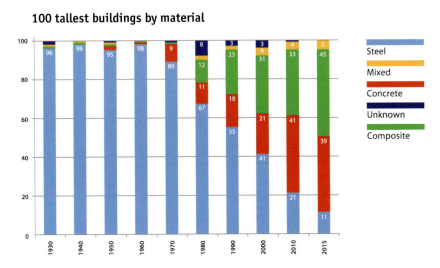

100 tallest buildings by material

← Figure 0.7:
100 tallest buildings by structural material each decade, from 1930–2015 (data as of January 2016)

This book is arranged in ten chapters, each covering particular issues associated with tall buildings. Various experts have contributed throughout to progressively illuminate the subjects under consideration. The first three chapters provide a backdrop to the issues surrounding city planning, tall building occupation and the political significance of 'changing the skyline'. The contributions from leading experts in the various fields range from thought pieces and philosophy to practical realities for occupiers and building managers. It is possible in these chapters to appreciate the special nature of a tall building and the particular factors that come into play in a far wider context than simply the appearance, design or internal space planning.

In the next four chapters, the guide explores the design, engineering and construction issues that are part and parcel of high-rise development. These sections are illustrated and supported by numerous examples and descriptions of completed projects, as well as some in the early stages of design. The advances in construction methodology and techniques, along with safety and site welfare, are also covered because the high-rise business has become more holistic than it was perhaps ten years ago.

The final chapters describe the significant and special matter of construction and potential deconstruction. A vision of the future concludes the book, to give an insight into what might happen in the UK and internationally in the tall building marketplace.

Perspectives on Building Tall

1

Any proposal for a tall building usually stirs up a range of strong emotions amongst public and private stakeholders, as well as within the development, design and construction community. At the early inception and concept stages interest tends to be focused on wider considerations than just the appearance and purpose of the building. In a series of thought pieces, this chapter highlights the issues around these sometimes controversial, ambitious, risky and expensive endeavours.

← *Future skyline of the City of London*

Contributors

Dr Antony Wood
Paul Scott
Peter Murray

Why Build Tall? | Dr Antony Wood

Drivers for building tall, such as land price, the desire for a greater return on financial investment, or the desire for an icon to 'brand' or promote a corporation or a city remain consistent. However, the need for denser cities as a response to climate change and more sustainable patterns of life has become an increasingly important driver in recent years.

Land prices and return on investment
Historically, the higher cost of land typical of city centres has always been a motivating factor for the construction of tall buildings. The higher land cost drives a need for the developer to realise a greater return on investment by creating more floor area for sale or rent. It needs to be noted that the greater return on investment through providing more floor area is obviously offset by the higher construction costs required of high-performing materials and systems at height, such that eventually a 'height threshold' of return vs cost will be reached.

Corporate branding and the global skyline
Whereas tall buildings have been used throughout their history as marketing tools to portray the vitality of a corporation, such as SwissRe (also known as The Gherkin) in London, now they are increasingly portraying the vitality of a city or country on a competitive world stage. This is reflected in the titles of the buildings themselves – previously endowed with names such as Woolworth, Sears or Petronas, they are now more likely to be named TAIPEI 101, Chicago Spire or Shanghai Tower. The buildings are being used to brand a city, since many cities, especially in developing countries, believe it necessary to have a signature skyline to be considered successful and thriving.

Rapid urbanisation and climate change
There are perhaps more compelling reasons for the increase in tall buildings than just corporate or urban branding. It is believed that there are now almost 200,000 people urbanising on this planet every day (United Nations statistics), requiring a new city of about one million inhabitants every week to cope with this global migration from rural to urban. In some places, this is an organic transition driven by the economic opportunities afforded by cities. In others, it is a combination of organic and political forces. In China, both existing cities and almost entirely new 'overnight' cities are mushrooming, as part of an official policy of urbanisation, changing the economy from one powered by manufacturing and agriculture to one powered by consumption. China now has more than 150 cities of one million people or more, and plans to move 250 million people into cities by 2020.

The classic model of a dense downtown working core with a massive, ever-expanding low-rise suburban periphery is an unsustainable one, due to the increased infrastructure needed (roads, power, lighting, waste handling, etc.), as well as the energy expenditure and carbon-emission implications of the home–work commute.

Cities need to become denser to create more sustainable patterns of life, reducing the horizontal spread of infrastructure networks and to be more efficient in land use, partly for retention of 'natural' land for agricultural purposes.

Although tall buildings are not the only solution to achieving high density in all cities, they can be part of the solutions for some cities. This urban-density driver, coupled with the city-symbolism/ iconic driver, has been influential in the escalation of the number of tall buildings being built and planned in developing countries.

Magnet Cities | Paul Scott

Why build tall? The explosive demand for tall buildings in the world's 'magnet' cities (see Figures 1.1, 1.2 and 1.3) reflects forecasts that, by 2050, 80% of the world's population will be living in cities. London's population is expected to increase from 8.5 million in 2015 to 11 million by 2050. In New York, the population will grow from 8.2 million to 9 million by 2040. And Shanghai's residents will surge from 24 million to 50 million by 2050. China's strategic urban plan is to create 100 new cities, each containing at least one million people [Hoornweg and Pope, 2014].

↓ *Figure 1.1:*
Shanghai's skyline

London and New York remain the ultimate examples of cities where the demand for residential and tall commercial/corporate towers are closely linked: these two cities are still the world's key financial reactor-cores, though Singapore and Shanghai are expected to join them by 2025. London and New York are also the most desirable cities to live in, particularly for the super-rich, or the merely wealthy.

↓ *Figure 1.2:*
London's skyline

↑ *Figure 1.3:*
New York's skyline
with the iconic
Empire State
Building

→ ↑ *Figure 1.4:*
Tall buildings
development
cycles in London

In cities such as London and New York, at least four factors are driving – and sometimes constraining – the design and construction of commercial and residential towers.

First, there is a central need to densify development to meet the increasing demand for residential and commercial accommodation from growing urban populations, and to maximise development on land whose values continually rise.

Second, the construction of these buildings must be timed to suit corporate and macro-economic liquidity-cum-investment cycles. Developers' decisions to build tall are based on their ability to meet actual or predicted demand.

Third, tower projects must fit the urban development strategies of the relevant planning authorities.

And fourth, the design of new towers must convey the required site- or use-specific image, which could range from corporate power to luxe living.

These four conditions can pressure one another, and tend to complicate the design and delivery of tall buildings.

Tall building cycles
The development of tall commercial or corporate buildings tends to proceed in clusters that concentrate particular kinds of activity and accentuate the image of specific parts of the city's skyline. But these developments are dependent on positive economic cycles, as the revealing record of tall building construction in central London shows, as seen in Figure 1.4.

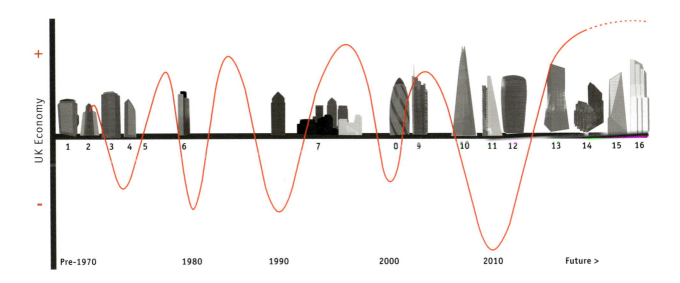

UK Economy

+

-

1 2 3 4 5   6   7   0   9   10   11 12   13   14   15   16

Pre-1970   1980   1990   2000   2010   Future >

Creating homes or foreign investment vehicles? Following the global financial crisis, the demand for tall buildings in London and New York is greatest from residential developers. Overseas investors are treating these particular cities as investment focal points, where property values appear to be in permanent acceleration.

In 2015 there were more than 250 tall buildings planned or under construction in central London [London Tall Buildings Survey, 2015], with premium housing developments concentrated along the River Thames from Canary Wharf (see Figure 1.5) to Battersea, or in locales such as Elephant & Castle, Paddington, or the City Road to Shoreditch urban segment (see Figure 1.6). These are generally premium housing developments towards the upper end of the market.

↓ *Figure 1.5:*
Canary Wharf,
London,
commercial
buildings and
new residential
development,
Newfoundland
Tower

↑ *Figure 1.6:*
Principal Tower,
London. Principal
Tower is a joint
development
by Brookfield
Property Partners
L.P., Concord
Pacific and W1
Developments

One of the greatest challenges faced by 'magnet' cities is how best to deliver tall residential buildings that are affordable to their steadily increasing home-grown populations. In London, the Greater London Authority (GLA) and the Mayor of London's '2020 Vision' identifies the need for 400,000 new homes, increasing to one million by the mid-2030s, in anticipation of an additional 450,000 new jobs by 2023 [Boris Johnson, 2013]. Predictably, the GLA's London Plan discourages development in outlying areas, and promotes greater urban densities around transportation nodes where tall buildings are generally encouraged.

Is planning an accelerator or a design quality filter?
Regulatory planning processes have a big effect on the quality of schemes for tall buildings. Compliance with planning policy is an established part of the design process and in most cases has led to designs that are contextual in their responses.

In some Asian and Middle Eastern cities, developmental speed is key, and their planning frameworks support this. If tall buildings of architectural merit are produced, it is often because the developers and architects involved are ambitious and push design quality to the limit. Of course, it should also be

noted that not all developers and architects of tall buildings are absolutely committed to maximum architectural quality and in these cases it is up to the planning authorities to demand it.

There are additional complicating factors in London, where there are 33 planning authorities, each with a different tall building policy. For example, in the City of Westminster, which has a strong economic base, a range of housing stock and a high proportion of designated Conservation Areas, tall buildings are limited to specific places, such as Paddington, which have good transportation links. Other boroughs, such as Southwark, encourage tall building developments in the wake of The Shard, as the catalyst of further regeneration and job creation.

Great cities have recognisable centres that are typically characterful, intense and vibrant. The risk, both architecturally and in terms of city image, is a cascade of tall buildings that have limited ambition, lack integrity and give little back to society in the form of public space or social infrastructure.

The very least that must be assured, strategically, is the design of tall buildings of the highest possible architectural quality. For this to happen there must be a concerted desire by those involved to do the right thing – socially, contextually and architecturally – but this does not need to be a threat to profitability.

Do We Need Icons? | Peter Murray

When New London Architecture (NLA) published its research findings in 2014 which showed that over 250 new towers were either under construction or in the development pipeline in the capital, the *Evening Standard* likened the results to 'Dubai-on-Thames', which presumably reflected the author's dislike of the rich mix of towers in the Emirate, made up of styles and forms that merge into a massive, muddled wall of steel, glass and concrete. Many of these towers are designed to be icons with innovative shapes and expressive structures, but because they are set in the context of others also fighting for attention, they lose their iconic status. The real icon of Dubai of course is the Burj Khalifa (see Figure 1.7), not just because it is tall but because it is tall in relation to the rest of the city. It stands out and has become a key part of the Dubai brand.

→ *Figure 1.7:*
The Burj Khalifa, Dubai

← *Figure 1.8:*
30 St Mary Axe,
London

Some suggest that iconic architecture is a new phenomenon, driven by modern marketing and branding, but ancient civilisations certainly understood the impact of large structures. By locating the Acropolis on top of a hill, the Greeks ensured it commanded the city beneath and became a powerful and universal advertisement for Athenian politics and culture. Equally, St Paul's Cathedral towered over a city ravaged by the 1666 Great Fire as a symbol of London's resurgence – and the protection of its views and its role as an icon – is key to controlling development to this day. Indeed, the Mayor's London View Management Framework and the St Paul's Heights legislation recognises that once a building has to start jostling with others for attention, it can lose that iconic status.

There is no doubt that the emergence of the elliptical form of 30 St Mary Axe on the London skyline had a substantial impact on international attitudes to London as a city, particularly in the Far East where the UK's image has always struggled to be separated from the Queen, corgis and half-timbered cottages (see Figure 1.8). It became an important image in the marketing of the Olympics both before and after the bid. It told the world that London was a modern city and proud of it.

Today London is recognised around the world by the London Eye, The Gherkin and The Shard as much as by busbies and Buckingham Palace. As the number of towers in the City cluster grows, people are beginning to complain that views of The Gherkin are being obscured.

A handful of star buildings may be a good thing for the branding of a city, but what about the rest of the tall buildings? With a few exceptions, most successful cityscapes work best when they exhibit an appropriate balance of the exotic and the more mundane. Dubai fails as a piece of city because too many icons are fighting for attention, whereas New York has spread its icons amongst the more mundane streets and avenues – The Empire State Building, the Chrysler Building, One World Trade Center and 8 Spruce Street (see Figure 1.9) enhance rather than fight with their surroundings.

It is not just about height, but it helps – the geometry of the 426m-high super-slender 432 Park Avenue in New York is restrained, yet its proportions, scale and its novelty will ensure its iconicity (see Figure 1.10).

Herzog & de Meuron's proposal for the Tour Triangle (see Figure 1.11) will be central Paris' first skyscraper for over 40 years and is a clear statement by the pro-development Mayor Anne Hidalgo that the city is throwing off its reputation as a museum city and is open for business. Her welcome of this new pyramid in Paris contrasts with statements in 2014 from Chinese President Xi Jinping who called for a return to classic architecture in China following on from the development of such buildings as the CCTV Headquarters tower designed by Rem Koolhaas in Beijing.

In Canary Wharf, Cesar Pelli's One Canada Square retains its iconic status as the pinnacle of the cluster of towers all with less interesting tops. The second phase of Canary Wharf, at Wood Wharf, will feature an iconic 'corn on the cob' tower by Herzog & de Meuron (see Figure 1.12); the circular plan, height and complexity of the façade set against a collection of more modest orthogonal structures confirm its status as a key identifier for the whole development.

In contrast, the redevelopment of King's Cross has eschewed such expressive architecture. This is hardly surprising since Graham Morrison of Allies and Morrison, who headed up the master planning team, made his views known in a speech entitled 'The Trouble with Icons' which he gave at the Royal Academy in 2004. 'What is the value of turning functional buildings into iconic ones? Are we simply trying too hard? Is a building's purpose compromised by its style?' he asked. King's Cross, of course, has a great icon in the form of St Pancras Station and the streets that are being developed around it create a robust backdrop to its Gothic exuberance.

In this era of Google Earth and global economics, new development and city skylines shape the external perception of cities, as well as the lives of their inhabitants. The contemporary city certainly has a need for icons – for buildings that stand out from the rest and reflect positive values of place. It just does not need too many of them!

↙ *Figure 1.11:*
The Tour Triangle, Paris

↓ *Figure 1.12:*
Residential tower at Canary Wharf, London

Occupier
Perspectives

2

← *Shanghai, China*

Contributors
Mat Oakley
Jenny
Mac Donnell

There has always been a human fascination in building tall, so where more natural to start in our efforts to design better tall buildings than with the occupiers who live and work in our current attempts and understand what does – and most importantly what does not – work for them? Occupier research and feedback provides a valuable insight into the most important aspects from the occupier's perspective.

The Fascination with Building Tall
Mat Oakley

The question of why office occupiers like tower space is a surprisingly difficult one to answer. One of the reasons is perhaps the decision has more to do with human nature than any particular economic or business rationale. Indeed, some psychologists have argued that the desire to be high stems from some atavistic desire in humans as predators to be able to see their prey from afar!

Whatever the driving force behind our need or enjoyment of being up high, it is clear that this is by no means a recent phenomenon, as we do have one example that still remains from ancient history – the Great Pyramid of Giza (see Figure 2.1). The fact that this structure, equivalent in height to a modern 40-storey office building, still remains after 4,000 years is impressive alone, but when you consider that the difference in height between the opposite corners of its foundations – which are more than 320m apart – is only 2cm, you have to marvel at the standard of the ancient Egyptian specification.

↓ *Figure 2.1:*
Great Pyramid
of Giza, Egypt

Jumping ahead around 3,900 years takes us to the evolution of the modern residential and office tower. Arguably, many of the residential towers of the 20th century have been demolished and condemned as a failed social experiment in moving the slums to the skies, whilst the office towers have stood the test of time much better. The guiding principle behind those first successful 20th-century office towers in Manhattan and Chicago is still the most true and easy to understand why occupiers like towers today: they are a practical solution to lack of developable land, and consequently very high land values. Indeed, the world's major clusters of towers still exist in locations such as Hong Kong, Tokyo and Manhattan, where land supply is naturally constrained by the local geography. Office occupiers that want or need to be in these markets arguably have little choice other than to consider an office tower; their only flexibility is around the height, specification and location of the tower that they end up occupying.

Why Locate in a Tall Building?
Mat Oakley

Having identified that occupiers choose towers in areas where the land supply is limited, we will now consider some reasons why occupiers choose tall buildings where they have more choices. This takes us towards more human aspects such as people, profile and status. Why does an occupier choose high-rise over low-rise in a relatively unconstrained city like London, Chicago or Shanghai? To get to the heart of this question we have to examine why occupiers choose one location or building over another. Most surveys of CEOs and property decision-makers point to the same important factors, namely location and availability of staff. In cities such as Shanghai, Chicago and London, the availability of staff is less of an issue but location within the city is important. Most surveys, including Savills' regular 'What Occupiers Want', point to rent being only the fourth or fifth most important factor in building selection. In the context of tower buildings, where the rents achieved on the top 25% of the building are almost always within 5% of the top rent being achieved in that market at that time, a flexible attitude to the rent bill is a fairly fundamental attribute for all occupiers considering high- over low-rise, but the first priority is to see if the leasing terms are within the organisation's budget. However, neither of those two key factors implicitly supports the decision to take office space in a high-rise office building. If we accept that really both factors of the CEOs are about the same thing (i.e. attraction and retention of staff), maybe the attractiveness of office space in tall buildings is being driven by the employees' preference for it?

Do staff like tall buildings? The BCO's 2013 'What Workers Want' report identified the top 15 most important factors to workers, and while tall buildings can deliver all of those, none were specifically factors that could only be delivered in a tall building.

1   Improve comfort (temperature, light, noise, smell)
2   Kitchen facilities
3   Improve security
4   Improve WiFi quality
5   Provide funky fit-out
6   More/better meeting rooms
7   Better break-out areas/increased provision
8   Improve/advertise 'green' policies
9   On-site café
10 Enhance/have more colour
11 Green space/roof terrace
12 Office art/greenery
13 Better/more shower and changing facilities
14 Better internal workplace flexibility
15 Bicycle storage

However, some of the factors, such as security, roof terraces, on-site cafes, natural light and general comfort, might actually be easier for the developer to offer in a high-rise than a low-rise building, purely as a function of the higher rent on tower space. Indeed, given that light is probably the most commonly complained about factor in pre- and post-occupation surveys, the height and generally smaller floor plate of a high-rise will often mean that more staff are close to a window than in an equivalent low-rise building (see Figure 2.2). Supporting this theory is Markel International's feedback that the quality of the light in its office space was a deciding factor.

While surveys and research are obviously the first call for a researcher, the question of why people like towers is probably best answered with the statement 'because they're high!' Many people like

high-level views of cities; witness the global market for high-level viewing platforms of various types. While the worker on the 44th floor may seldom look out of the window, they seem to like the idea that it is there, and perhaps more importantly the impact it has on visitors to their company or desk. Telling people that you work in a landmark building is probably less likely to lead them to glaze over than telling them you work in a vanilla low-rise (at least until a newer, higher, better landmark is built). As the 2015 'Skyscrapers' report by Knight Frank handily sums up, 'they are seen as a way to give staff a workplace that feels special'. So if the building choice is about staff attraction and retention, then making your staff feel special seems like a very good reason to go high.

Practicalities

Many organisations seem to love the higher specification and larger ground floor lobbies that often come with towers. This is lucky because with the challenges of the lifting strategy in tall buildings, they may be spending longer in the lobby than they are used to. Actually, while the wait for lifts tends to be a hot topic of discussion when an occupier is new to a building, the toxicity of this usually diminishes fast. Indeed, a recent arrival to one of Shanghai's' latest crop of towers said, 'we actually find that the lift lobby has become the new water-cooler, the place where staff from different teams get to pause, meet

↑ *Figure 2.2:*
Sky Lobby,
Shanghai Tower

and swap ideas'. The feedback from the occupiers has generally been positive about the lifts and people often used the time spent waiting for one as thinking time.

The only consistent negative, and area of surprise, that we hear associated with tall buildings is around evacuation. Prior to a move to a high floor, how many organisations check that all of their staff can actually walk down 40 floors of stairs? The CFO of a business that has recently taken the top floor of one of London's towers commented: 'I was surprised how many people had bad knees from sport when we had our first practice evacuation.' Of course this is why we have evacuation plans and practices, but perhaps occupiers considering tower space in the future might want to be a bit more searching when they survey their staff prior to the move. Markel International found that some of its staff was feeling anxious about evacuation times; however, as it was a relatively new occupier of a tall building, it expected this matter to settle down in time.

An Insider's View | Jenny Mac Donnell

A further aspect to consider is the perspective of individual organisations and their reasons for selecting the tall buildings. Two office occupiers and the manager of a tall building shared their experiences of occupying tall buildings.

Cathy Yang, General Manager, Shanghai Tower Leasing and Operation Company Limited
Cathy Yang manages Shanghai Tower, which at 632m is the tallest building in China and the second tallest in the world. Previously, she managed TAIPEI 101, formerly known as the Taipei World Financial Center. It was the world's tallest building from 2004 until the opening of the Burj Khalifa in Dubai in 2010.

William Poole-Wilson, Perkins+Will, North Wabash Avenue, Chicago
(and Principal of PBP+W London)
William Poole-Wilson is Principal and Regional Practice Leader at Perkins+Will. A company of architects, interior designers, urban designers, landscape architects, consultants and branded environment experts, it is a global practice with an office in Chicago on North Wabash Avenue which was renamed AMA Plaza in 2013.

Andrew Davies, Markel International, 20 Fenchurch Street, City of London
Andrew Davies is the Chief Operating Officer at Markel International, a subsidiary of a US-based holding company for insurance and investment operations around the world. Markel International is an international insurance company which looks after the commercial insurance needs of major businesses, SMEs, professionals and sole traders. It is based in 20 Fenchurch Street, London. Markel moved in spring 2015, and they have leased three floors totalling 7,000 sqm. This table sets out the details of the tall buildings occupied and managed by these organisations:

BUILDING	ARCHITECT	CONSTRUCTION COMPLETED	DATE OCCUPIED	STOREYS	HEIGHT (metres)
Shanghai Tower, China	Gensler	2015	2016	128	632
330 North Wabash Avenue (renamed AMA Plaza in 2013) Chicago, USA	Ludwig Mies van der Rohe	1972	1994	52	212
20 Fenchurch Street, London, UK	Rafael Viñoly Architects	2014	2014	36	160

A questionnaire was shared with the three contributors and follow-up interviews were conducted via email, by telephone and in person. The aim was to identify how they went about selecting the right building to occupy and the various factors that had weight in that decision process.

The selection process
Cathy Yang from Shanghai Tower works with a number of organisations when they are going through the selection process. She believes that when a business is searching for a new office, the factors that the senior management consider are the location, leasing terms, building image, convenience and so on. When a tall or supertall building is on the property list for selection, the decision-making dynamics may change because there may be different factors to consider. The decision-makers may place greater emphasis on the tall or supertall, and the first priority is to see if the leasing terms are within the organisation's budget. Alternatively, the management team may refuse to consider a tall or supertall building because they personally dislike

them. For many organisations, the leasing terms are the deciding factor when selecting a new office but, setting that aside, the companies that favour a move into a tall or supertall building generally value the specific benefits of being in a tall building such as the view, the image, etc.

Markel International considered a number of other buildings and selected its space in 20 Fenchurch Street because of the size and shape of the floor plate and the amount of light in the space. Perkins+Will chose its space because it is a landmark building in Chicago which the company feels is closely aligned with the purpose, vision and values of its architectural practice.

The view and light levels
Yang believes the view is usually the most important selling point from a leasing perspective. Offices in tall buildings offer panoramic views of the city that lower buildings find difficult to compete with, and this is a major attraction. In this age when creativity and innovation are of vital importance to a company's further development, it is likely that the openness and broadness of the unobstructed view is helpful to staff productivity.

↓ ↓ *Figures 2.3 and 2.4:* **The view from Markel International, 20 Fenchurch Street, London**

For Markel International, the light in the office space was the most important factor in selecting 20 Fenchurch Street (see Figures 2.3 and 2.4). The open-plan layout of the floor plate and low number of private offices ensures everyone has access to daylight, allowing staff to work in the office without artificial light.

Image For Cathy Yang, a supertall building is often the landmark and most recognisable building in the city. No doubt image is why many companies choose to be located in tall buildings. It also gives credibility to the companies inside the tower. The office address, especially for Asian supertall buildings, can enhance corporate image for less prominent companies and this helps to increase the rental levels of supertall buildings.

For Markel International, the image is that of a successful company operating in a landmark building, which assures its clients that they are going to be around for the long term. It gives the business a sense of permanence and stability, helping to promote it in a competitive marketplace.

Perkins+Will is located in a landmark, tall, Mies van der Rohe building in Chicago. The company feels that this location is pertinent to its business as architects, and projects its image as experts in modern architecture.

↓ *Figure 2.5:*
AMA Plaza,
Chicago

Large floor plates Cathy Yang finds that for companies occupying a large space, their preference is to be on as few floors as possible. In most cases tall and supertall buildings offer large floor plates and large-scale occupiers are able to occupy a smaller number of floors, facilitating a more efficient organisation and management of their different departments. Markel International also credits the large floor plates as being a key factor in its decision to locate in a tall building. It leases the largest floor plates in the building to accommodate its staff on as few floors as possible. Perkins+Will is leasing a tall building for the same reason; being on just two floors enables better communication across the business and offers more flexibility for the adjacencies required.

Connectivity Markel International, our London occupier, is attracted to tall buildings because of the improved connectivity within the organisation. Markel has added a central staircase in its space at 20 Fenchurch Street to improve the connectivity across their three floors (see Figure 2.6). The combination of the open-plan space and London views make it simpler for colleagues to locate each other as they have easy points of reference to use because of the clear sightlines of London's landmarks; e.g. 'Frank is the person facing St Paul's.'

↓ *Figure 2.6:*
Interior staircase at Markel International, 20 Fenchurch Street, London

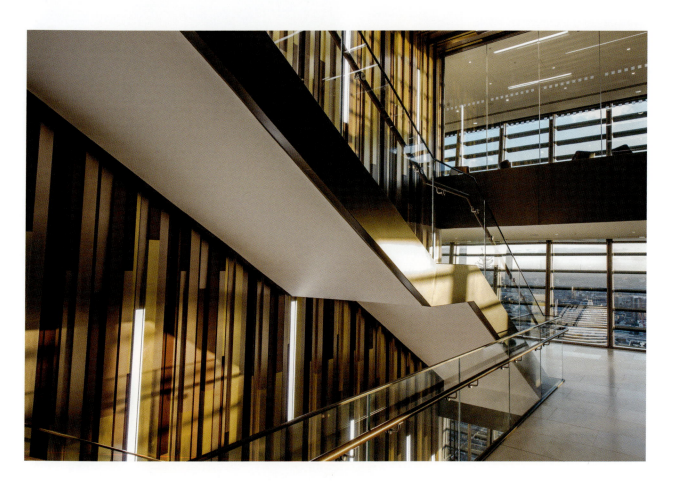

In Chicago, Perkins+Will occupies a tall building with large floor plates which facilitates improved connectivity across the business. It allows a productive layout of the space and communication efficiencies across the business because of the space plan. Improved connectivity helps to drive through good protocol and attitudes in the office.

Safety concerns From the perspective of Yang, there are clear concerns associated with occupying office space in supertall buildings (see Figure 2.7), especially regarding fire safety. Potential occupiers often require a detailed explanation of how fire prevention and fire safety systems work. It is important that the building manager can demonstrate there is a thorough safety and security plan, and emergency response procedures in place.

Markel International finds that some of its staff feel some level of anxiety from being located in a tall building. Initially, the response to fire alarm tests has been immediate evacuation. However, after a few false alarms resulted in people making for the emergency stairs straight away, the staff are now more willing to wait for the announcement to leave the building.

Vertical transportation

For Yang, the question often asked is whether the occupier can reach their floors using one lift rather than needing a sky lobby or transfer. The lift is the piece of equipment that receives the most complaints (often closely followed by the air-conditioning system). The developer must make sure the vertical transportation system is efficient. The building manager then has to make sure that the lifts are well maintained and operated (for a more detailed analysis and explanation on lifts in tall buildings, see Chapter 5). This applies equally to the cooling systems. Markel International has mixed experiences of the lifts in its building. There are longer waits than usual at peak times – such as lunchtime – but generally there are few significant issues. At first, additional support was provided to some staff members to manage their anxieties over the height of their office space and the lift speeds. These concerns are easing as people become accustomed to their new location.

Perkins+Will finds that the lifts are not as quick and efficient as it would like. Holding events where a large number of people arrive at the same time is a challenge but this is also a result of the security checks within the building. Furthermore, the firm has a preference for faster lifts with destination control because of the increasingly dense occupation of its office space.

Brand recognition

In Yang's view, a supertall building could easily have over 100 tenants. There may be more than one large occupier in such a building. Opportunities for brand recognition for the occupiers are more limited than in a smaller or low-rise building, often restricted to a signboard outside the building. A large occupier can sometimes acquire the naming right for the office building they occupy, but this is rare – the Willis Tower in Chicago is an exception rather than the norm. Most owners of supertall buildings would never give a company the naming right. Yang feels that overall, as tenants move into supertall buildings they enjoy the privilege and benefits of being in these famous landmarks and individual branding becomes less important.

Markel International is one of a number of occupiers in 20 Fenchurch Street where the policy is to limit company branding to the individual company reception floors (see Figure 2.8). The company is happy with this policy, as it is located in an iconic tall building with an instantly recognisable address and good security facilities.

Perkins+Will's branding is restricted to its own space and it ha a preference for some branding for its organisation at the ground floor level, so that visitors to the building can see the branding in the reception area.

↓ *Figure 2.8:*
Reception, Markel
International,
20 Fenchurch
Street, London

Amenities/convenience From the amenity perspective, Yang considers the larger site area, often accompanied by a podium, encourages retail outlets and other amenities. Acknowledging the consumer potential of the large number of occupants, the podium provides for food and beverage retailers, convenience stores and even fashion or luxury stores. Occupants do not need to leave the building for their daily needs and this can be an attraction for busy office workers.

For Perkins+Will, the availability of amenities was not a factor in its decision to locate in a tall building. Markel International provides staff with a café on the 25th floor, the lowest of its three floors (see Figure 2.9). It has also provided a large open-plan entertaining area on this floor to allow them to hold functions in-house. It found it had more visitors to the new office as people were keen to see the space, particularly as it is in a new landmark tall building. The building also provides a bar and two restaurants in a sky garden at the top of the building, which are open to both occupiers and the public.

↑ *Figure 2.9:*
Café*, *Markel International, 20 Fenchurch Street, London

Conclusions | Jenny Mac Donnell

It is clear that many businesses see the benefits and value of occupying tall and supertall buildings, often for relatively hard-to-measure reasons. People have an ongoing fascination with tall buildings, choosing to occupy them as they see advantages for their organisation's workforce, profile and status. They are prepared to pay high rents for this space, and the vacancy rates in high-rise buildings are generally lower than in low-rise buildings. Working in a landmark building is also seen as attractive to employees, which helps organisations to recruit the best people.

As the occupier interviews show, the process of selecting a new office location varies but the size and shape of the floor plate, the amount of light and image are all common factors to be considered. Each occupier attributed better connectivity and communication across its business to the large and efficient floor plate. A lot of the attraction has to do with image and brand recognition, but then so does much of what we spend our money on today. As building technology, vertical transportation and safety systems improve, we will undoubtedly continue to build higher and higher, and there are definitely tenants who are attracted to towers in locations where companies and people are happy to pay to feel special.

The Urban Fabric

3

Many capital cities around the world exist because they provide the commercial, cultural and intellectual attraction that people want in a successful city and have become a perpetual engine of re-invigoration and legacy. To survive and be successful, a city needs to evolve, develop and expand. This naturally promotes population growth, which requires vertical expansion to prevent urban sprawl. This chapter looks at regeneration and the importance of the public realm in the creation of new urban fabric and communities.

← *Convoys Wharf, London*

Contributors

Nigel Bidwell
Colin Wilson
Eric Parry

Urban Regeneration | Nigel Bidwell

Urban development and regeneration requires a high degree of integration between land use, transport, economic development and identified development plans at regional, sub-regional and city levels. In the UK, an important innovation in urban regeneration in the 1990s was the evolution of a city-wide perspective, recognising that leadership, vision, policy development initiatives and partnerships with key stakeholders to business, local community and governance are fundamental to successful regeneration strategies. The integration of tall buildings to areas earmarked for regeneration can change land value; economic potential which in turn can increase investment in the infrastructure system.

Regeneration potential
The critical mass of large-scale tall building developments can lead to significant changes to the city's social, environmental and economic conditions. When they are used as part of a wider area regeneration or comprehensive redevelopment, they contribute by promoting economic potential, social opportunity, and diversity and positive change through identity.

The final point is less easily quantified but of psychological significance. Cesar Pelli's One Canada Square in Canary Wharf, London, has become synonymous with the city's second financial district, its pyramid form, stepped shoulders and reflective stainless steel representing the free market and a new confidence (see Figure 3.1). Importantly, it also symbolises the opening up of the closed confines of the docklands to become a publicly accessible part of the city.

This approach is mirrored at Convoys Wharf, Deptford (see chapter opener on p. 30) with the cluster of tall buildings marking the public opening up of the walled compound that was formerly Henry VIII's dockyard and the gifting of the riverfront back to the people. Meanwhile, at Old Oak Common, north-west London, the proposed tall buildings will provide an identity, in particular from mid-range and long-distant views marking the new town centre on the horizon.

↓ *Figure 3.1:*
Canary Wharf,
One Canada
Square, London

Placemaking Architects' engagement in designing and building tall buildings in Britain came to the fore in the 1950s and 60s through the mass social housing policies of that period and the much admired Corbusian ideals of lifted buildings with open space, light and air. The insistence of architects in this period to adhere to strict 'rules' of orientation often set these buildings at odds with their surrounding street patterns, dislocating them from their context and leaving poorly defined spaces and little sense of streetscape (see Figure 3.2).

After time, in parallel with their physical disturbance and poor contribution to placemaking, came their social rejection driven by their aesthetic, often poor-quality construction and underfunded maintenance strategies. Interestingly, and at odds with European and Asian societies, our tall buildings are the domains of the two differing ends of the social spectrum, with living at height still associated with social housing but also now the very rich.

The challenge for the tall buildings of the modern era is to work with the street edge, help define space and respond to context. Tall buildings are a complex typology, needing to deliver on many fronts from their role on the horizon to their integration with town centres to their immediate engagement with streets and spaces.

Consider also the environmental impact of tall buildings. It is well known that tall structures can detrimentally affect wind conditions at street level caused by increased wind speeds creating down-draughts and turbulence. Solutions to this can include canopies or setbacks to counter these downdraughts but perhaps a more comprehensive solution would be to create podiums on which tall buildings sit. The added advantage of this is the reduced urban scale of the urban block facing the street and a more sensitive street scale edge to incorporate mixed-use activity (see Figure 3.3).

↑ *Figure 3.2:*
Church Street residential blocks, London

↓ *Figure 3.3:*
One Excellence, Qianhai

Active frontages, retail, commercial or cultural uses add to the street level experience for pedestrians and building occupiers alike. A sensitive composition of tall buildings around a well-considered public space can create a unique setting for urban interaction because the tall buildings can provide the intensity of residents and building users to keep the space vibrant throughout the day and evening.

The Rockefeller Center is a good example of a carefully considered grouping of tall buildings around the public realm that has active frontages, active use and interest in the public space, and is further enhanced with public art. The result is an iconic space that is renowned worldwide (see Figure 3.4).

Governance controls and planning policies

The evolution of high buildings' policies recognise their urban sensitivity due to their impact and scale. The differing European approaches have been translated into planning policy with different characteristics, as indicated by the following examples:

- Frankfurt's strategy is set according to City Government objectives and designates building height zones, which reinforce its radial structure and increase density at traffic intersections. Three high-rise cluster areas are being promoted with guidelines for street level activities, open space and parking. Outside these zones and the Central Business District (CBD), building height is limited to 20m.

↓ *Figure 3.4:*
The Rockefeller Center plaza, New York

- Rotterdam's policy is set according to Metropolitan Government objectives, with an emphasis on strategic policies of containment and consolidation of high buildings to two zones alongside development of appropriate infrastructure. Development control tools include zoning, height controls, character areas and the establishment of a discussion forum focusing on innovation in practice.
- Paris' policy is set according to City Government objectives, with an emphasis on containment of high buildings to specific, defined and limited zones within the city and on the city fringe, with high buildings being permitted provided they adhere to specified guidelines. Within the old centre, building height is limited to 6 storeys, set out by Haussmann to a fixed datum but at La Defense there are no height limits.
- London's policy is shaped by the London Plan and core strategy policies. Tall building provision is controlled by the strategic views framework safeguarding view corridors from strategic points across the city to St Paul's Cathedral and Westminster Palace, controlling height within specific zones, and varying policies within the boroughs that have their own definition of height.

New York and London illustrate that the difference in the timeline of city formation shapes different and contrasting directions towards governance controls and planning policies. New York follows a strict zoning policy as compared to London's organic architecture, planning and heritage response.

New York, with its recognisable city grid pattern, is planned around a well-organised series of city blocks. The heights of the city blocks were not controlled until the erection of the 42-storey Equitable Building at 120 Broadway in 1915. The detrimental environmental impact this building had on its neighbours highlighted that there were no controls on coherent city planning and governance regarding height, shadowing and sunlight. This became the catalyst for the zoning resolution of 1916, which established height and setback controls, designated residential districts and fostered the iconic tall, slender towers that came to epitomise Manhattan.

The zoning resolution was reconsidered in 1961, dramatically reducing residential densities at the city fringes, encouraging incentive zoning and the development of plazas and street vistas, further coordinating use and bulk regulations, incorporating parking improvements and emphasising the use of open space.

New York is divided into basic zonal districts for residential, commercial and light industrial. These are further divided into a range of lower-, medium- and higher-density districts. These are overlaid by special purpose zoning districts tailored to the unique characteristics of the city, such as commercial overlay districts and Limited Height Districts that impose height limits in certain historic districts designated by the NYC Landmarks Preservation Commission.

London is the direct opposite to the New York model. Instead of the regimented grid form, it is the epitome of the medieval multi-organic city whose character, complexity and polycentric urban evolution has been developed through time, layering and identity.

London, like New York, faces the challenge for growth, transport, economic development, housing, culture, infrastructure and climate change but, unlike Manhattan, has fewer tall buildings, therefore each new tall building proposal appears to carry a greater significance in the urban setting. Pressures on location and siting are influenced by the building's proximity to conservation areas, listed buildings and their settings, registered historic parks and gardens, scheduled monuments, the Green Belt or Metropolitan Open Land, World Heritage Sites or other areas designated by boroughs as being sensitive or inappropriate for tall buildings.

City Densification and Placemaking – London, A Case Study | Colin Wilson

The skyline is politics

Planning policy and guidance need to be considered in their political and economic context. That the skyline is politics is apparent to anyone with an understanding of a city's history. In one view of Tower Bridge (see Figure 3.5) you would see the Norman Tower of London dominate a conquered city, HMS Belfast, designed to protect the trade of a mercantile city, and in the distance the towers of Canary Wharf, the physical articulation of economic liberalism and itself a challenge to the monopoly of the City of London's previously pre-eminent office core.

London's politics and approach to planning are unlike those of Paris, Berlin and New York. The British planning system is discretionary, with each case considered on its own merits within a broad strategic framework. This differs significantly from the zoning approach of New York or the Paris designation of a single district to house tall buildings. Arguably, London sets a higher benchmark for developers to pass and provides a more varied skyline with the old being mixed with the new against the backdrop of a more dynamic economy.

Planning policy for tall buildings is never only a technical and aesthetic consideration. Current strategic planning guidance for London was initially set out in the 2004 London Plan. Strategic

↓ *Figure 3.5:*
Tower Bridge, Tower of London and HMS Belfast with Canary Wharf buildings in the distance, London

governance of London had only been re-established in 2000, with the intent of providing strong political leadership to a city which had lacked it since the closure of the Greater London Council in 1986. By 2000 it had become clear that London was at a competitive disadvantage with other world cities that had the benefit of strong city-wide governance and political direction. The intent of the first elected Mayor of London, Ken Livingstone (2000–08), was to re-establish London as a premier world city, and part of his plan to achieve this was to explicitly promote tall buildings as a way of sustainably delivering jobs, homes and an 'Urban Renaissance' through city densification as championed by the then national government and the architect Richard Rogers.

Planning for tall buildings before 2000
The majority of tall building policies in the London Boroughs plans in 2000 had their genesis in the Greater London Development Plan (GLDP) of 1976 where three categories of tall building locations were identified through a sieve analysis. The first was areas in which high buildings were inappropriate (such as close to areas of special character like the Tower of London or with relationships to major parks); the second was where tall buildings might be considered sensitive (such as riverside locations or close to other heritage assets); and the third was areas not covered by the other categories and therefore potentially appropriate for tall buildings.

The considerations were entirely aesthetic and based on an assumption that to see a tall building in the context of existing historic locations was a bad thing. London, like many cities, has a rich and extensive built heritage and as a consequence this guidance limited the locations that could accommodate tall buildings to generally places in which nobody wanted to build them, particularly when the population and economy of the city was contracting. This policy approach persevered in London until replaced by the 2004 London Plan policy, some 28 years later.

Wider considerations
What this policy approach entirely missed were the wider considerations of sustainable city development and, in particular, proximity to existing and planned public transport, to brownfield regeneration sites and to areas in need of regeneration. Tall buildings could play a part in delivering the Urban Renaissance in London and other UK cities, not just as part of a beauty parade but as key drivers of a city's economic revival. Crucially, rather than taking a value neutral approach to tall buildings, the policy was to actively promote them as a reflection of London's political and economic resurgence.

Policy 4B.9 of the London Plan 2004 'Tall Buildings-Location' stated that:

The Mayor will promote the development of tall buildings where they will create attractive landmarks enhancing London's character, help to provide a coherent location for economic clusters of related activities and/or act as a catalyst for regeneration where they are also acceptable in terms of their design and impact on their surroundings.

The policy went on to advise that boroughs may wish to identify areas that may be sensitive to tall buildings but, importantly, they should not 'impose unsubstantiated borough wide height restrictions'. The Mayor was aware that there would be some resistance to his promotion of tall buildings, but considered he had the democratic mandate to promote them and was entitled to do so through his London Plan.

The 2008 London Plan, also under Mayor Ken Livingstone, took an almost identical policy position. In May 2008 Boris Johnson became Mayor and part of his campaign had included the need to rein-in the active promotion of tall buildings. Under the new mayor, the London View Management Framework was reviewed and strengthened, as were policies in relation to the protection of London's heritage. Nonetheless, tall buildings, though no longer actively promoted, were still identified as 'playing a role' in development. Much of the remainder of the policy in relation to Opportunity Areas and the Central Activities Zone (CAZ) and areas of regeneration remained in place, as did the tests of good architectural quality. The latest London Plan, published in 2015, sets out in Policy 7.7 that 'Tall buildings should be part of a plan lead approach to changing or developing an area by the identification of appropriate, sensitive and inappropriate locations.' This is not quite a return to 1976,

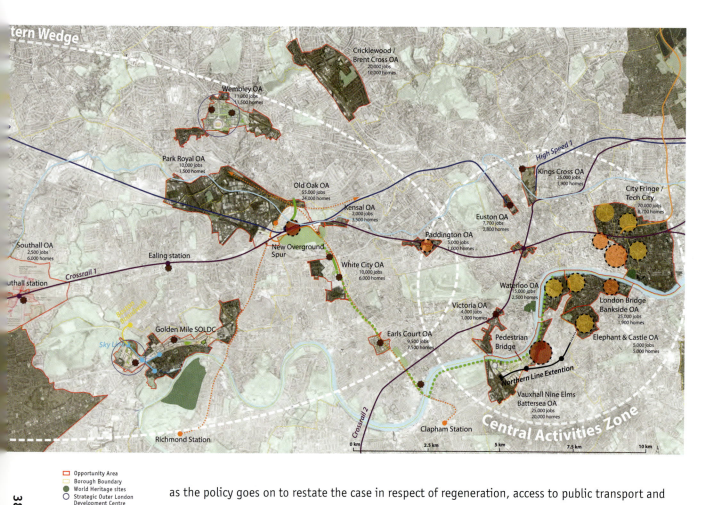

Cricklewood /
Brent Cross OA
20,000 jobs
10,000 homes

Wembley OA
11,000 jobs
11,500 homes

High Speed 1

Park Royal OA
10,000 jobs
1,500 homes

Kings Cross OA
25,000 jobs
1,900 homes

City Fringe /
Tech City
70,000 jobs
8,700 homes

Old Oak OA
55,000 jobs
24,000 homes

Kensal OA
2,000 jobs
3,500 homes

Euston OA
7,700 jobs
2,800 homes

Southall OA
2,500 jobs
6,000 homes

Ealing station

Paddington OA
5,000 jobs
1,000 homes

New Overground
Spur

White City OA
10,000 jobs
6,000 homes

Crossrail 1

uthall station

Waterloo OA
15,000 jobs
2,500 homes

London Bridge
Bankside OA
25,000 jobs
1,900 homes

Victoria OA
4,000 jobs
1,000 homes

Golden Mile SOLDC

Earls Court OA
9,500 jobs
7,500 homes

Pedestrian
Bridge

Elephant & Castle OA
5,000 jobs
5,000 homes

Sky Li

Northern Line Extention

Crossrail 2

Vauxhall Nine Elms
Battersea OA
25,000 jobs
20,000 homes

Richmond Station

Clapham Station

Central Activities Zone

0 km   2.5 km   5 km   7.5 km   10 km

Legend:
- ☐ Opportunity Area
- ☐ Borough Boundary
- ● World Heritage sites
- ○ Strategic Outer London Development Centre
- Existing tall building cluster
- Emerging tall building cluster
- Proposed tall building
- Proposed tall building cluster
- New Parks
- Green Grid Connections
- Overland

as the policy goes on to restate the case in respect of regeneration, access to public transport and concentration in Opportunity Areas and the CAZ.

There were – and are – many commentators who maintain that there was no need for tall buildings in London and that there is no demand. The demand soon became apparent over the course of the early 2000s. In 2015 there were proposals for more than 250 tall buildings in London, of which 80% were residential, the remainder being offices. The vast majority of these buildings were conceived within the context of London Plan policy and were in locations the plan identified for tall buildings.

Identifying locations

The Mayor undertook to work with boroughs to identify locations for tall buildings, particularly within the CAZ and the London Plan Opportunity Areas, the latter being the large brownfield development sites that had been created as a result of London's de-industrialisation. The CAZ and the Opportunity Areas were to become the key areas in which clusters of tall buildings were promoted within the Mayor's Opportunity Area Planning Frameworks and within the London boroughs' local plans (see Figures 3.6 and 3.7).

The CAZ contains two world heritage sites, numerous listed buildings and many conservation areas. In addition, the Mayor has the London View Management Framework that protects key strategic views (see Figure 3.8) across London to St Paul's and the Palace of Westminster.

London Plan policy clearly sets out that tall buildings had to be considered in relation to context and so when planning for the location of tall buildings, consideration had to be given to the layering of a number of policies,

↑ *Figure 3.6:*
London's tall buildings' sites in the Western and Central Activities Zones

→ ↑ *Figure 3.7:*
London's tall buildings' sites in the Eastern Zone

→ *Figure 3.8:*
Sightline from strategic viewpoint on Primrose Hill, London

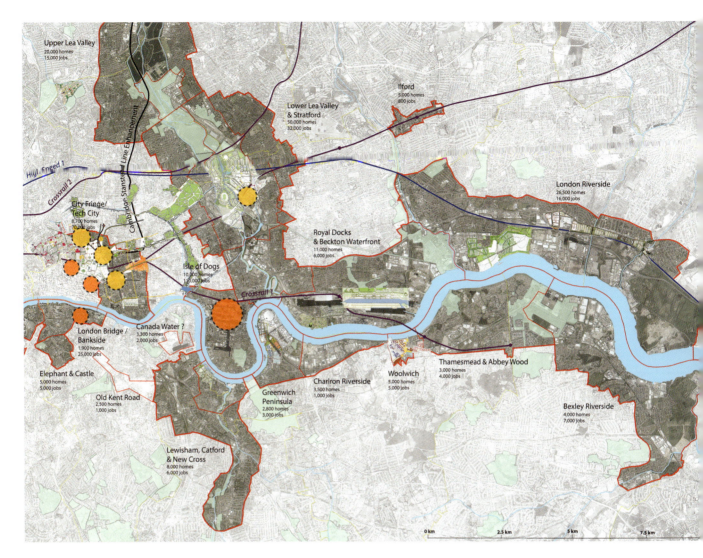

Upper Lea Valley
20,000 homes
15,000 jobs

Ilford
5,000 homes
800 jobs

Lower Lea Valley
& Stratford
50,000 homes
32,000 jobs

London Riverside
26,500 homes
16,000 jobs

High Speed 1

Crossrail 2

Cambridge-Stansted Line Enhancement

City Fringe/
Tech City
8,700 homes
70,000 jobs

Royal Docks
& Beckton Waterfront
11,000 homes
6,000 jobs

Isle of Dogs
10,000 homes
110,000 jobs

Crossrail 1

London Bridge /
Bankside
1,900 homes
25,000 jobs

Canada Water ?
3,300 homes
2,000 jobs

Thamesmead & Abbey Wood
3,000 homes
4,000 jobs

Woolwich
5,000 homes
5,000 jobs

Elephant & Castle
5,000 homes
5,000 jobs

Charlton Riverside
3,500 homes
1,000 jobs

Old Kent Road
2,500 homes
1,000 jobs

Greenwich
Peninsula
2,800 homes
3,000 jobs

Bexley Riverside
4,000 homes
7,000 jobs

Lewisham, Catford
& New Cross
8,000 homes
6,000 jobs

0 km   2.5 km   5 km   7.5 km

of the areas designation within CAZ or an Opportunity Area, of its proximity to public transport provision, and of its potential impact on heritage assets such as the World Heritage sites at the Palace of Westminster and the Tower of London.

Opportunity Area
Borough Boundary
Existing tall building cluster
Emerging tall building cluster
Proposed tall building
New Parks
Green Grid Connections
Overland

Example: Vauxhall Nine Elms Opportunity Area Planning Framework

Vauxhall Nine Elms is an Opportunity Area, and in the 2008 London Plan was also designated as part of the Central Activities Zone. In parallel, it was de-designated as a Strategic Industrial Location (SIL). Rather than wait for developers to come up with their own plans in response to this change of use, the GLA worked with the London Boroughs of Lambeth and Wandsworth to develop a comprehensive planning framework for the area. This work was undertaken by the GLA's planning team rather than an external consultant, a conscious decision aimed at building-in house skills and retaining close control over the project (see Figure 3.9).

The plan began with the change of use, and on the basis of this change a development capacity study was undertaken and this was framed by an overarching idea about a park and open space structure for the area, comprising the formation of a linear park linking the two major existing metropolitan parks at Battersea and Archbishop's Park, a river walkway and a series of new connections to the river for existing residential communities to the south and north via a new footbridge. The tall buildings would therefore contribute to the delivery of the targeted development capacity and the delivery of the open space network. The tall buildings would not be ends in themselves but rather a means to an end, that being the creation of a high-quality extension to the city that would integrate open space, public transport and tall buildings.

English Heritage undertook a study of the area's development and extant character, and the GLA team mapped the strategic and local views, conservation areas and listed building locations and, importantly, the setting of the Palace of Westminster World Heritage site. A 3D digital model of the area and its wider city setting was then used to test options for the location and height of tall buildings

↓ *Figure 3.9:*
Nine Elms tall building strategy, London

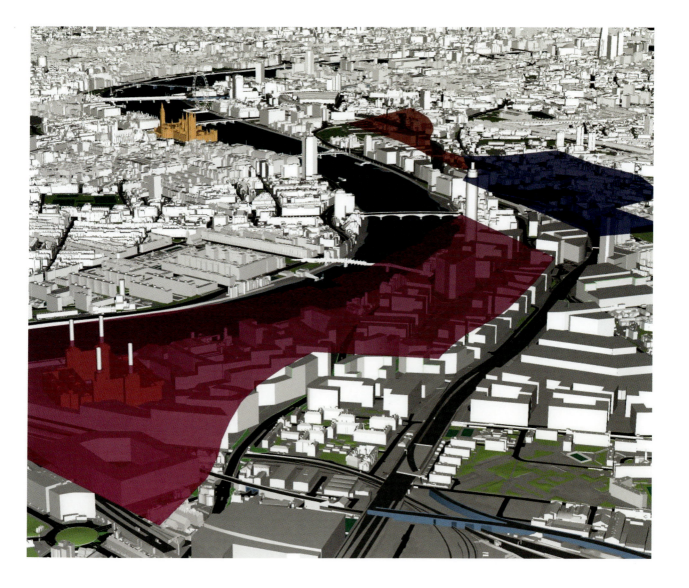

and to assess their potential impact on the World Heritage Site and on their more immediate context. How this impacted on overall development quanta and on transport infrastructure was also tested. A series of options was then taken to the Mayor and the Deputy Mayor for Planning, Sir Simon Milton, as well as to the leaders of Lambeth and Wandsworth, and a consensus was reached about the extent of the tall building cluster at Vauxhall and the broad parameters in respect of its height and composition, with the consented but not then built Vauxhall Tower, at 180m expected to form the pinnacle of this new cluster, with other buildings being of a height of about 150m (which had been consented at appeal in 2004 ahead of all other development). It was agreed by the respective politicians that this would be the basis on which the plan would be consulted with the wider public.

The public realm strategy for the area clearly set out the contributions landowners were expected to make to the delivery of the linear park, but it was less prescriptive about the design of individual tall buildings. The approach taken was that as long as individual tall buildings fitted within the broad parameters of location and height set out in the framework, and as long as they delivered their part of the overall public realm strategy, then the detailed design and use of the buildings would be a matter for individual design teams. However, given the site's location close to a World Heritage Site, the tall building designs would be expected to be of the highest quality and, in aggregate, as schemes came forward would be expected to have regard to each other to ensure that the overall cluster composition produced an attractive skyline. The planning framework set out that a wall of development was to be avoided and this was partly obviated by the need to deliver the linear park, which provided separation between tall buildings in the heart of the cluster.

This resulted in a plan that provides a strong but flexible discipline. This approach allows for individual design teams to make their own creative contribution to the delivery of the wider planning framework by avoiding being overly prescriptive. It also avoids a plan that reflects the ideas of a single master planner at a single point in time. Nobody is able to predict the future or have all the best ideas, but as a public authority the GLA provided the context in which others can creatively contribute to the delivery of a longer-term vision.

The Public Realm | Eric Parry

There is no more important issue in designing tall buildings than their impact on the surrounding public realm. Tall buildings are notoriously antisocial in terms of their presence on public space. As landmarks, they naturally stand out rather than 'blend in', they create wind turbulence rather than acting as buffers, they cast long shadows and with relatively tight footprints they have a much greater portion of their perimeter given over to servicing demands than lower buildings. Set against the potential negatives are the equal and opposites of the city icon and the greater densities that nurture the animation of the public realm.

A design discussion on public space should begin with the sensory world of light, sound, smell and touch, coupled with what we do in public: meet, greet, eat, meditate and, above all, take time out from work. Create an impenetrable curtilage, a guarded service bay, a wall of pulsing louvres or too much arid open space and it is all too easy to snuff out any desire to linger – which is the best litmus test of a successful public place. With global competition increasing, city authorities are now alert to the fact that unless these fundamentals of civility are in place, migration will naturally follow. There are many ways of reconciling tall buildings and their context but three strategies merit highlighting.

1 Integrate the base of the building(s) in mediating scaled urban fabric – examples being the Commerzbank Tower (Kaiserplatz 1) in Frankfurt designed by Foster + Partners, completed in 1997 (see Figure 3.10), and The Shard, London by the Renzo Piano Building Workshop, completed in 2013.

→ *Figure 3.10:*
**Commerzbank
Tower, Frankfurt
by Foster +
Partners**

→↑ *Figure 3.11:*
**Proposals for
new office tower,
1 Undershaft,
London**

→→ *Figure 3.12:*
**Raised base of the
proposed building
at 1 Undershaft,
London**

2 Levitate as much of the building's base as possible to allow passage through and vistas beyond – examples being the Daley Center in Chicago designed by C.F. Murphy Associates, completed in 1965, and The Leadenhall Building (122 Leadenhall Street, London) designed by Rogers Stirk Harbour + Partners and completed in 2014. Neighbouring the Leadenhall Building, the proposed new tower at 1 Undershaft will feature a public square at the base, creating a new urban realm (see Figures 3.11 and 3.12).

3 Allow the sculptural form of the tower to define its base and create a focus for the public realm – examples being the structural web of 30 St Mary Axe, London by Foster + Partners at the centre of a newly defined urban space (see Figure 3.13).

↑ *Figure 3.13:*
30 St Mary Axe,
London

A framework plan that creates the dialogue of many towers to accumulatively reinforce a broader idea of public realm is critical for the 21st-century city. Frankfurt has conceived a grand promenade of tall buildings; the city of London an artificial topography from a 'summit' to 'foothills'.

Whilst banishing tall buildings from historic settings safeguards the silhouette and urban character of the historic city, it denies the excitement of juxtaposition and density. Radical changes of scale are nothing new, as the towers and bulk of medieval cathedrals bear witness, and it is salutary to realise that Haussmann's Parisian boulevards would be cut-out film sets without the historic fabric into which they were savagely inserted.

For a cluster of tall buildings laid onto a medieval urban grain, such as in the case of the City of London, it is important that as the three-dimensional jigsaw puzzle tightens its grip on available space, the public realm is preserved. Rights of light envelopes should not be the determinants of urban form; public space should be. The Rockefeller Center in New York remains one of those brilliant precedents, creating a relative calm and three-dimensional theatricality at its very public central space. The plaza has become a famous tourist destination, offering ice-skating during the winter (see Figure 3.4). The Center was also prescient in its invitation to the public to view the city from its observation deck by creating roof gardens. The advent of the sky lobby and innovative vertical transportation means that there is a now well-established tendency of multi-levelled public realm and mixed-use towers.

The critical balance lies between the needs of a successful public realm to be porous, informal, stimulating and varied with the needs of tall buildings, with their population of thousands requiring thresholds that are carefully supervised, clearly outlined and constantly monitored.

A good balance can only be achieved by reconciling apparently conflicting requirements to be mutually supportive and beneficial.

Tall Building Clusters | Nigel Bidwell

Many cities in the world have tall building clusters because of their zonal planning policies. American cities have their 'downtown' clusters, Frankfurt has its business district. Manhattan and Hong Kong could be considered as mega-clusters and are composed of an urban fabric containing a majority of tall buildings. In cities that are generally of lower scale, tall buildings take on a greater significance because they stand out above the general fabric.

Modern London has evolved as a polycentric city and has financial clusters such as the City and Canary Wharf but is now developing additional clusters, no longer solely made up of larger floor plate office buildings. These increased numbers of centres of activity have so far been sufficiently spread to naturally create groupings or clusters that punctuate the skyline. Any elevated view from South London clearly shows the building clusters of Canary Wharf, the City, Southbank and Nine Elms, and there are more on the way, not least Old Oak Common.

These clusters arise from multiple landowners' desires to build significant tall buildings in areas of opportunity, designated as such by policy or promoted by the commercial market. The combination of multiple owners and multiple expressions can result in an 'architectural zoo', creating a cluster of independent buildings of various designs often competing with each other for attention. In some instances, these have a self-regulating order but these informal ties can be stretched and broken. 20 Fenchurch Street steps away from the traditional city cluster and sits close to the water's edge, changing the character of this stretch of the Thames (see Figure 3.14). Meanwhile, in Vauxhall the rapidly growing cluster appears to have a shifting centre and seems a consequence of opportunity rather than true town planning.

↓ *Figure 3.14:*
20 Fenchurch
Street, London

More established townscapes, such as Manhattan, Hong Kong and Singapore, have many tall buildings and, because of the sheer number, a large number are 'background' buildings, part of the general urban landscape rather than a specific signifier of an urban event or celebration. New developments in China, more akin to the scale of city-making rather than site development, have provided new opportunities for planned compositions of towers. Large tracts of land in single ownership or with a single delivery vehicle provide the opportunity for planned clusters where the interrelationships between tall buildings and their profile in local, medium and long distance views

can be controlled. This approach could confine architectural expression, but with sufficient themes and controls and with an overall consideration for composition, many designers can be involved in the creation of the cluster, resulting in the whole being greater than the sum of its parts (see Figure 3.15).

London's Opportunity Areas, supported by the necessary infrastructure, have the chance to deliver planned clusters. Few examples of note exist in the city, with the exception perhaps of the Barbican towers (see Figure 3.16) and the Worlds End complex, but the Earls Court and Old Oak Common Opportunity Areas have the ownership and planning vehicles that allow for a consciously-placed family of tall buildings whose strength in form comes from their composition and architectural quality.

← *Figure 3.15:*
The skyline of Qianhia

↑ *Figure 3.16:*
The Barbican Estate, London

Design

4

Building Design:-
- Building facade:
- shape
- material
- structure
- sustainable features.

...sign of tall buildings requires close collaboration amongst a team with a wide range of expertise and experience to produce high-quality and well-executed results. The involvement of the client is crucial. The building core and space efficiency are critical to vertical accessibility, safety and the economics of the product. The façade is particularly critical and often warrants disproportionate attention. This chapter looks at a number of design-related topics that need to be coordinated and optimised to achieve success.

← *56 Leonard Street, New York City*

Contributors

Lukasz Platkowski
Steve Bosi
Greg Dunn
Colin Roberts

Space Planning, Flexibility, Efficiency and Connectivity

Lukasz Platkowski

The discussion about tall buildings is shifting from construction matters, such as shape, façade, materials, structure and sustainable features, to its urban context, community integration and positive impact on the end user. Truly sustainable tall buildings result in towers that may be occupied 24 hours a day, blending the border between living and working, and putting emphasis on end-user requirements, behaviour and wellbeing.

Building typology Tall buildings can generally be divided into three families:

Residential and hotels: define and focus on user experience, where possible integrating local culture and inviting communities in. Good designs capitalise on outward views and allow visitors and residents to interact with nature by introducing operable windows, large balconies, winter gardens and loggias. 56 Leonard Street, designed by Herzog & Meuron, uses interlocking glass villas to provide views of the city and extensive external spaces (see chapter opener on p. 48).

→ *Figure 4.1:*
The New York Times Building

Commercial offices and headquarters: innovative schemes focus on their tenants' need to recruit a dynamic, more creative and collaborative workforce, whose preference for buildings that map to organisations' values puts a premium on sustainability, wellness, connectivity and locations that are active, transit friendly and walkable. The New York Times Building, designed by Renzo Piano Building Workshop and FXFowle Architects, provides connectivity through every floor of the building by using internal stairs (see Figure 4.1).

Mixed-use: create community clusters incorporating retail, offices, hotels, residential apartments and public amenities. The mixed-use typology creates 24-hour destinations and encourages user interaction and collaboration. At The Shard, designed by Renzo Piano Workshop, the public viewing gallery provides unforgettable vistas across London.

There are increasingly greater similarities between these building typologies, with the features traditionally associated with residential and hotel towers often being found in commercial offices, headquarters and mixed-use buildings.

Efficiencies in tall buildings
Building efficiency measured by calculating net-to-gross area ratio is dependent on several characteristics of a development:

- typology
- height
- shape
- floor plate size
- number of users
- amenities
- internal atria
- lifting strategy
- fire escape strategy
- floor-to-floor height
- structure
- MEP systems
- local building codes, etc.

It is not possible to give exact target values for building efficiency; however the following indicative guidelines may be applied:

BUILDINGS BELOW 300m	Residential / hotel: 80%-90% Commercial: 75%-80% Mixed-use and headquarters: 70%-80%
BUILDINGS BETWEEN 300-600m	Residential / hotel: 75%-85% Commercial: 70%-80% Mixed-use and headquarters: 65%-75%
BUILDINGS ABOVE 600m	Defined by the CTBUH as the 'megatall', these structures are commissioned to become a landmark representing a country, city, community or organisation. They are the least efficient, accommodate several uses and their efficiency fluctuates at around 60%.

Workplace design: the new metrics that matter?
Good workplace design adds value to an organisation's bottom line. It is widely acknowledged that approximately 20% of the cost of running a typical organisation lies in the real estate area (capex, rentals, maintenance, security, etc.) with the remaining 80% being employment related costs.

The more intangible metrics associated with the impact of good workplace design measure reduction of sick days, training costs, employee attraction and retention, and perhaps most importantly, employee satisfaction, engagement, productivity and innovation. These concepts, whilst more difficult to measure, are arguably the most important for an organisation to evaluate.

The most innovative and effective workplace design begins with a carefully considered floor plan configuration, layout and flexibility to support requirements of the diverse tenants. Tall buildings cater for large amounts of office space and innovative, responsible schemes consider end-user needs from the early stages of design.

Effective space planning
The term 'space planning' describes the layout of the office floor, including:

- the combination of cellular offices
- open-plan working
- collaboration zones
- support spaces, such as meeting rooms
- café/hub zones
- print areas
- server rooms
- stores, and circulation routes.

↓ → *Figure 4.2:*
**Office Tower,
Saudi Arabia**

Optimum spatial planning zones are typically 3:2 in width to depth ratio (see Figure 4.2). Large, rectangular, column-free spaces with a 1.5m internal grid are considered to be the most efficient and supportive of diverse tenants. To allow for the maximum flexibility, floor plan depth should range from 10.5m to 15m from the external envelope to the core wall. Nine metres is considered to be the absolute minimum depth for efficient planning. In this Saudi office tower, designed by Gensler, a pre-concept stage space plan investigates two workplace scenarios of the 13.5-m deep floor plan: a cellular office plan and fully open plan.

A typical floor, usable for a single tenant, should be easy to sub-let without negative impact on the internal efficiency. Figure 4.3 shows a study of the typical floor sub-let options of two, four and eight tenants per floor, with shared amenity space in the centre of the building.

↓ *Figure 4.3:*
**KAFD WTC Tower,
Riyadh**

→ *Figure 4.4:*
**Centre-split core,
KAFD WTC Tower,
Riyadh**

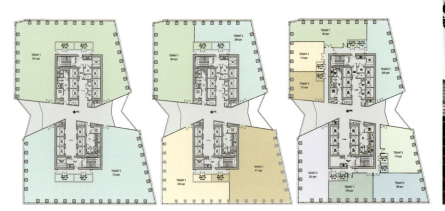

End-user focus Internal communication and work environment can be enhanced by good design. Tall buildings designed with consideration of the likely occupier provide employees with a choice of spaces that enhance their focus, collaboration, learning and socialising, resulting in increased productivity.

Non-centric core location Historically, incorporating a central core was the only way to design structurally sound tall buildings but today's technology allows the positioning of the core where it is most desirable from the occupants' perspective, although a central core still provides an effective solution for residential and hotel towers, where external views are of the most importance. Figure 4.4 shows a core design solution that creates three-storey community areas in the heart of the building, with direct access to natural daylight.

New ways of working require conducive spaces that provide flexibility, visual and physical connectivity, and support employee communication and collaboration. A core located in the centre of the floor plan is the least desirable solution from the tenant's perspective, as it becomes a physical separation for workers on the floor. Flexibility to design for on-floor collaboration may be achieved by splitting the core, offsetting the core from the centre or relocating the core to the perimeter of the building. Figure 4.5 shows how the location of the core on the north face of the building allows the creation of a large, flexible floor plan and unlocks the central space for break-out areas to support internal communication.

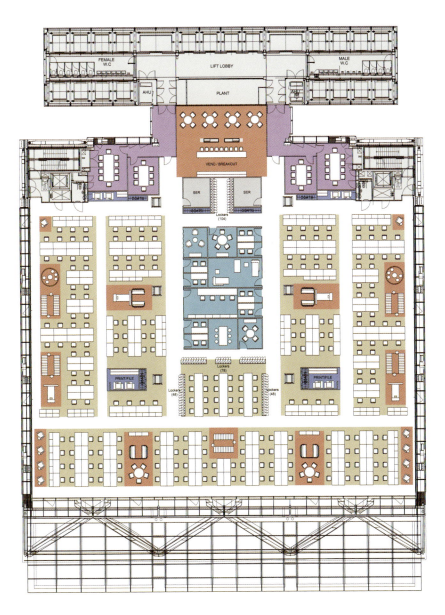

← *Figure 4.5:*
Aon's offices at
122 Leadenhall
Street, London

Connection and openness In headquarters towers, vertical connectivity between floors is as important as on-floor flexibility. The direct implication of the core relocation from the centre is an opportunity to introduce internal atria that bring in daylight, support natural ventilation and, by connecting floors, allow for inter-floor flexibility, employee interaction and communication.

Internal atria are a common solution in headquarters buildings; however there are also examples of floor cut-outs through a number of levels in speculative office towers to provide an ideal self-contained headquarters environment for a larger single tenant, or co-working space for multiple tenants who are open to collaboration and interaction with other businesses. Figure 4.6 shows an internal atrium connecting three floors, ideal to cater for large (30,000 sq ft) tenants. However, smaller organisations concerned with visual privacy may find this solution challenging.

Speculative office buildings need to cater for the needs of tenants occupying single and multiple floors, and the introduction of knock-out panels designed into the floor offers the flexibility to introduce interconnecting stairs after building completion (see Figure 4.7).

→ *Figure 4.6:*
Heron Tower,
London

↓ *Figure 4.7:*
The New York
Times Building

↘ *Figure 4.8:*
Garden in the
centre of the
building and
multi-use hall
at The New York
Times Building

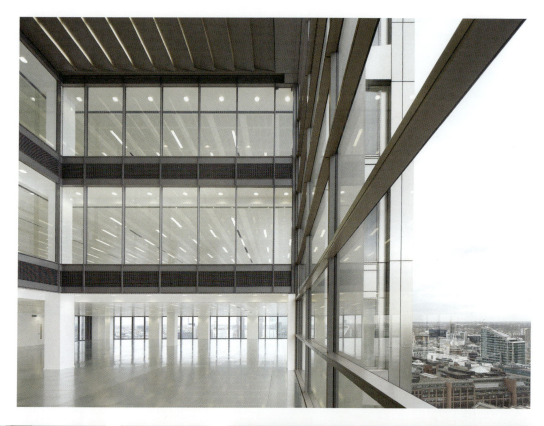

Shared amenities Amenities that are shared among tenants allow for further communication and collaboration, promote creativity, connectivity, effectiveness, wellbeing and sense of belonging to the community. This includes not only gyms, cafés and restaurants but also meeting rooms rented by the hour, theatres, auditoria, etc. Buildings become known for their public spaces, sky lobbies and viewing platforms (see Figures 4.8–4.11).

Natural ventilation Natural ventilation, typically achieved through considered façade design, which is evolving from weather screens to high performing, multi-use components of the building, has a direct impact on tenant wellbeing. Large areas of a typical façade require an amount of repetition; however there are opportunities for unique, bespoke solutions. Figure 4.12 shows a double-skin façade: a natural ventilation system that has a glass outer weather and air barrier and an inner layer with automated air vents, a wood curtain wall and manually operation sliding doors.

↑↑ *Figure 4.9:*
Restaurant at
The New York
Times Building

↖ *Figure 4.10:*
Public sky lobby
at Shanghai Tower

↑ *Figure 4.11:*
Sky garden at
20 Fenchurch
Street, London

Today façades are capable of greater interaction with the external environment, are an energy-harnessing tool (PV panels integrated into the envelope, capturing solar energy), and can support natural ventilation. The idea of connecting with the outside is becoming increasingly important. Technology development now allows for movable/foldable external walls to connect internal areas with the natural environment.

Mixed-use towers

Mixed-use towers are becoming the most innovative, responsible and iconic tall building designs; driven by the need of cities, communities and end users, they create a recognisable brand that inspires urban integration. The focus of mixed-use design is on creating vertical cities – communities of several typologies stacked on top of one another, interconnected and interacting through shared amenities.

Traditionally measured efficiency of a mixed-use development will typically be lower than a single-use tower, due to the vertical transportation requirements. However, this building typology is acknowledged to have the most positive impact on the community. It is occupied 24 hours a day and caters for multiple types of occupiers and the public, blending the distinctions between work, life and play, and encouraging public interactions.

↓ *Figure 4.12:*
The Tower at PNC Plaza, Pittsburgh

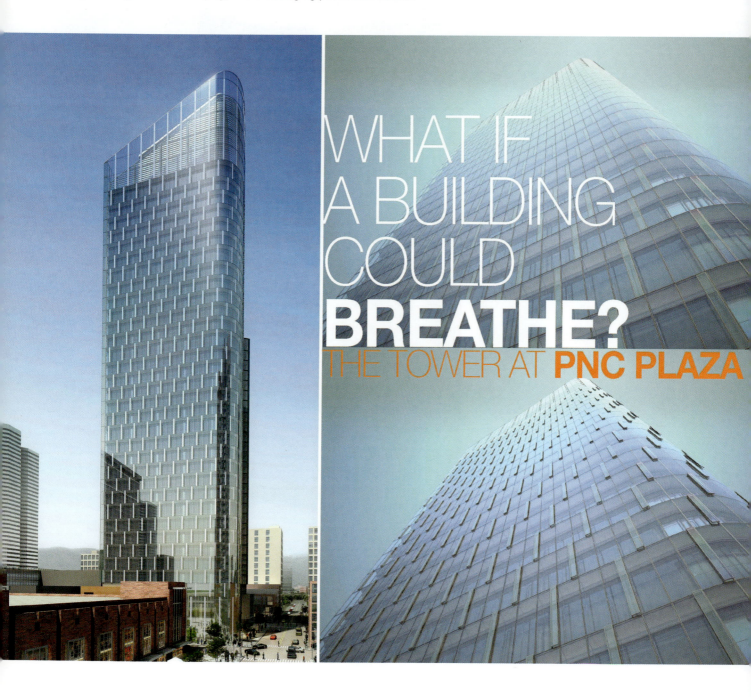

WHAT IF A BUILDING COULD **BREATHE?** THE TOWER AT **PNC PLAZA**

Façades | Steve Bosi

A building's façade can account for 25% of the build cost and carries the highest risk in terms of building performance and procurement, and ultimately it is what the public sees.

The need to thoroughly interrogate the client's brief should form part of the design team's objectives, to perfect it into a finely tuned set of requirements. Sometimes these requirements can conflict with each other, so a 'best fit' solution is often necessary.

Cladding/structure interaction
Whilst every structural engineer will strive to design an economical structure, the issue is emphasised when designing tall buildings. The repetition of floors and the need to reduce foundation loads across a concentrated area means that the structure is usually designed to its limits in terms of strength. Whilst this approach may generate savings, it is also important to understand how the structure will behave in terms of movement and how this will affect the cladding.

The range of structural movements that the façade needs to accommodate, whilst at the same time remaining weathertight, is a complex interaction of many factors. As the façade is typically supported from the edge of the floor plate, the behaviour of the edge beams play a primary role. These factors require that the cladding designer understands the structural behaviour of the supporting structure as well as an appreciation of any sequencing operations during the construction.

One particularly important point when designing for seismic performance in certain parts of the world is to define, at the outset, the level of performance that the cladding is expected to provide post-event. Provided that the cladding remains serviceable in the short term, accepting a degree of damage may give the best balance in terms of cost versus probability of the event occurring.

Procurement and contractor selection
The procurement route is typically dictated by the economic cycle. The supply base for high-end curtain walling products is limited and in times of high activity the focus is on securing a cladding contractor that has suitable design and manufacturing capacity which is aligned with the overall project specific construction programme.

Traditionally, the design has been fully developed but recently there has been more focus on getting a cladding contractor involved earlier, perhaps on a two-stage tender process. This is where a number of façade contractors tender against a set of preliminary information and then perhaps two of the most favoured are asked to fine-tune their offer during a second stage tender against a more comprehensively developed set of information.

An alternative to this has been the Pre Contract Service Agreement (PCSA), where a cladding contractor – or sometimes two contractors – are taken on for a specific period of time to develop the detail design. A design fee is normally paid by the client and this is offset against the contract value if the contractor is successful. This has the advantage that the detail design can be developed during the PCSA in conjunction with the client's design team and this provides a higher level of cost certainty. Refer to Chapter 7 for more procurement and market considerations.

Buildability
For high-rise construction, the cladding is generally fabricated in pre-assembled panels for attachment to the edge structure. These are typically assembled in the factory and this generally guarantees a higher standard of manufacture when compared to a site assembly process. The panels are transported to site where they are moved vertically to their destination floor by crane, hoists or manipulators.

Maintenance, replacement and access
For high-rise buildings located in city centres on congested sites, where there is minimal access provisions both during construction and afterwards, it is important to develop an access and maintenance regime that ensures that the external face of the façade is accessible not only for regular cleaning but also for occasional

replacement of components if necessary (see Figure 4.13). There is also a typical requirement in façade warranties that requires them to be cleaned at regular intervals in order to maintain the guarantees on the metal finishes which is an activity over and above regular window washing.

→ *Figure 4.13:*
Example drawing of system for access and maintenance to the external façade

For the remainder of the elevations, it is necessary to provide a building maintenance unit (BMU) on the roof or concealed within part of the façade. This arrangement requires a carefully integrated design, taking into account the proximity of any plant and amenity spaces, such as rooftop terraces. Given these sometimes conflicting requirements, the actual machines are often of bespoke design (see Figure 4.14) for the particular building in question. For tall buildings with plant spaces at interim levels, it is not unusual to locate additional BMUs in these locations.

→ *Figure 4.14:*
Example drawing of bespoke BMU solutions required by many tall buildings

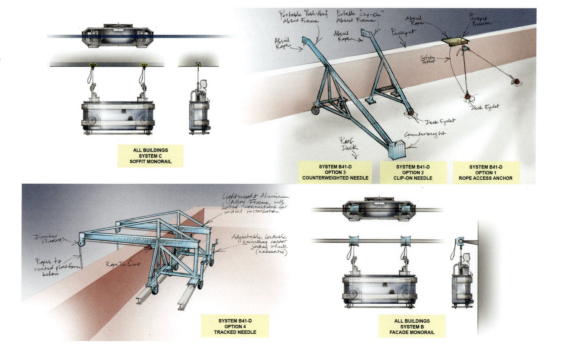

Aesthetics High-rise office cladding systems have something of a stereotype image. Partly influenced by the planning grid which is frequently a 1.5m module in the UK and differs slightly elsewhere, it is frequently a façade made almost entirely of glass (see Figure 4.15).

The 1.5m module provides a cost-efficient solution for the glass since there is little wastage from the jumbo flat glass pane of 6m x 3m.

When viewed from the inside, glass spanning from floor to ceiling is, rightly or wrongly, something of a given and whilst some designers question the need for so much glass, citing some understandable reasons, for now it remains a major component of the elevation.

← *Figure 4.15:*
Glass high-rise
cladding system

↑ *Figure 4.16:*
111 West 57th
Street, New York by
JDS Development

There is a need to balance the solar gains against cooling loads and natural light against artificial light, especially in deep plate layouts, which is why a best-fit solution is often required and the façade has to play its part in this.

In residential buildings the need for privacy results in a more protective façade. An example of which is 111 West 57th Street, New York, where the living areas facing Central Park are all glass with the bedrooms on side elevations being terracotta and bronze latticework over the glass (see Figures 4.16 and 4.17).

Future advancements

A fundamental limitation with cladding systems to date is that they are essentially static elements whilst they have to act in response to changing climatic conditions. The term responsive/adaptive façade has been used for some time now, occasionally in an incorrect context, but systems such as double skins do provide a degree of seasonal control by modifying the air flow inside the cavity, either actively or passively. The inclusion of blinds also provides for active control over solar gains.

The major components of a curtain walling system are glass and aluminium, and both of these have a relatively high-energy footprint. Whilst it is difficult to see a replacement for glass in the short to medium term, there are materials that could replace aluminium in the not too distant future. The primary candidate for this could be carbon fibre reinforced plastics. Until recently they were available in basic shapes only but recent advances now enable the extrusion of profiles not dissimilar to what can be done in aluminium.

Where glass is concerned, and in the context of commercial limitations, solid state switchable technology is probably the next step in controlling light and solar gains. The ability to pass a current over a glass coating in order to change its optical properties is not new but the limitations on sizes are only recently beginning to be overcome.

← *Figure 4.17:*
111 West 57th
Street, New York by
JDS Development

Cores | Greg Dunn

In any tall building, the cores must accommodate the overall engineering strategy whilst achieving the vertical transportation systems required to meet the owner's brief. They must also provide occupancy safety while satisfying the client brief and relevant building codes.

The optimum core design achieves these often competing elements with the most efficient arrangement that considers the core placement and geometry, specific design requirements of the various core elements, flexibility for future tenant requirements and constructability.

Specific tenant requirements may also drive core design, such as limitations on doors around the core perimeter and spaces to be built internal to the core, such as IT rooms, kitchens or specific security requirements.

Core arrangements should always be tested in the early stages of design for their efficiencies with multi-tenant arrangements for all but the smallest floor plates (below 600 sqm) to ensure the design incorporates the appropriate flexibility.

Core placement and geometry
There are a number of factors which may drive the core placement and the geometry, such as:

- Lease spans: the lease span is a very important tenant consideration and so the client brief may be very specific on these dimensions, which may influence the idealised core location.
- The size of the floor plate as dictated by the site or building design is a major factor. On smaller floor plates the core may need to be pushed to the side to achieve optimum lease spans on other elevations.
- Certain types of tenants may want very large areas of open space, which drive specific solutions. In this case, the required distribution of core elements may influence the core arrangement.
- Occasionally a site constraint will drive the core placement, such examples being a road or a subterranean tunnel under a building that prevents the main core from being located there.

Once any constraints have been identified, the next step is to consider various core typologies.

Core typologies
There are a wide variety of core arrangements for office buildings. However, these can be generally characterised as centre cores, side cores and distributed cores.

- Centre cores allow idealised lease-spans around the entire building. Centre cores can be easier to plan efficiently because the entire perimeter can be used for core elements that need access to the floor plate, but can restrict communication across a floor. Refer to the section *'Space Planning, Flexibility, Efficiency and Connectivity'*, at the beginning of this chapter on pp. 50-56.
- Side cores can be beneficial either on smaller floor plates to maintain decent lease spans, on larger floor plates to create larger fields of open spaces, and on buildings with a party wall condition to make best use of the building aspect. Side cores can reduce cladding costs and improve building energy performance by removing a glazed wall. They can also work well for servicing strategies that need outside air on a floor-by-floor basis.
- Distributed cores may be required on large floor plates to meet code or MEP distribution requirements and can also aid reducing storey heights by limiting the services' horizontal distribution.

Core elements
The relative drivers for the specific elements of core design are the local building regulations, local market conditions (as guided by organisations such as the BCO) and the client brief. For a diagram of typical core elements, refer to Figure 4.18.

Core structure
Core structure is either concrete or steel (or a hybrid) and may be different to the structure used for the rest of the building. Core structural walls or bracing lines (if required) should be as continuous as possible across the core. The core perimeter structure usually needs careful consideration, given the necessity for core elements and services to pass onto the floor plate.

Passenger lifts
Lifts are a major core element that usually work best planned 'deeper' in the core, with access via lift lobbies onto the floor plate. It is important to consider all of the non-typical floor arrangements, such as transfers, overruns and machine room levels, and ensure residual space left from low-rise lift banks that fall away is recaptured as valuable floor space at the upper levels (see Figure 4.19). For more information on vertical transportation systems, see Chapter 5 (pp. 83-87).

Other core lifts
The core will need to accommodate dedicated-use goods lifts, VIP lifts and other specific-use shuttles to serve special amenity spaces. Goods lifts need to be planned carefully to consider how they are accessed at loading bay level and will often form part of a plant replacement strategy. Ideally, goods lifts should be located together in order that they operate as a system.

Similarly, the access to VIP or other special dedicated use lifts need careful consideration although they can be 'buried' within the core in their express zone. Fire lifts within fire-fighting shafts need planning around the associated stair arrangements.

Stairs and fire-fighting shafts Stair numbers and arrangements are driven by both travel distance requirements and occupancy numbers. Ideally, the stair widths and planning will meet both of these requirements without one overriding the other. Stairs may require hardening and careful location relative to core structure for particular security considerations and they are often suited to being planned 'deeper' into core areas.

↙ *Figure 4.18:*
Core elements

↓ *Figure 4.19:*
Lift groups falling away at higher levels to release net lettable area

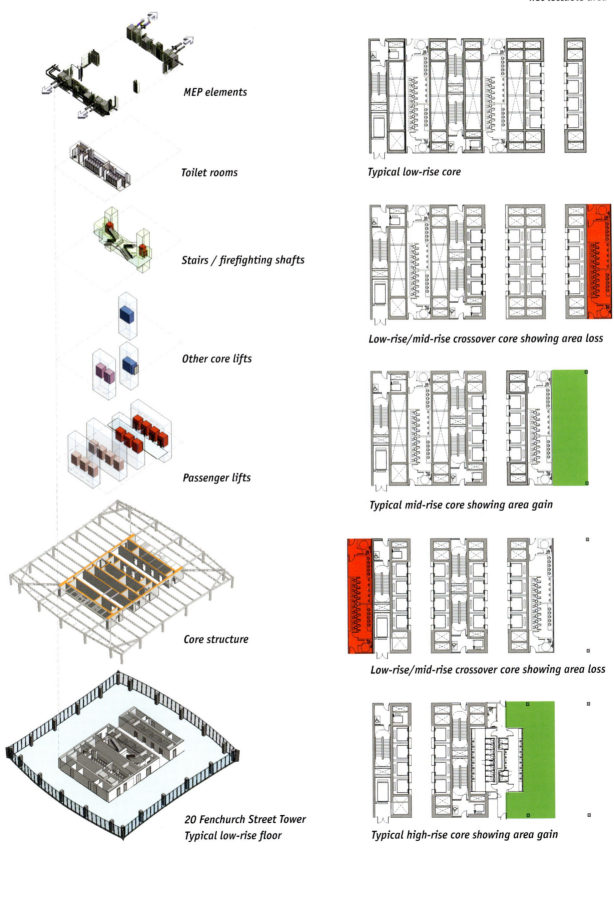

MEP elements

Toilet rooms

Stairs / firefighting shafts

Other core lifts

Passenger lifts

Core structure

20 Fenchurch Street Tower
Typical low-rise floor

Typical low-rise core

Low-rise/mid-rise crossover core showing area loss

Typical mid-rise core showing area gain

Low-rise/mid-rise crossover core showing area loss

Typical high-rise core showing area gain

DESIGN **63**

Toilet rooms Toilet fixture counts are usually provided to code requirements on the density specified in the brief. For many towers with multiple lift banks, the most efficient planning of toilet accommodation is by utilising inactive lift lobbies to make use of the constrained deeper core space rather than using up valuable lettable area.

Building services Building services risers are either 'express' risers that do not need to access into the floor plate on every level (examples include condenser pipes and generator flues) or risers that serve the office space on every level (such as IT, electrical and air supply and extract risers). Express risers are generally dimensionally consistent for the height of the building and are located in deeper space within the core, provided they can be planned to exit the core on the basement and upper plant levels they serve.

Accessible risers are often planned around the perimeter of the core with direct access to the floor plate and they require detailed coordination with structures to ensure adequate outlets onto the floor. For air risers that service the floor, locating them on core corners allows ductwork sizes to be kept to a minimum, allowing improved coordination with the building structure.

Perimeter risers can create significant access issues from tenant areas, so internal risers with good access to the tenant areas via lobbies and corridors can be considered to reduce the access requirement from tenant areas

Fire Safety | Colin Roberts

A fire safety strategy is an essential component of tall building design. As buildings get taller, the fire strategy takes on an even greater significance as it inevitably takes longer to escape and the consequences of a fire can be greater.

The main consideration in these strategies is therefore time. The engineer must show that all occupants can evacuate the building without being unreasonably exposed to the fire.

Codes Wherever the location of a tall building, there will be local or national code requirements and guidance, which will result in a compliant solution. These are likely to lead to unnecessary costs which can be avoided if a more risk-based fire engineered approach is adopted which takes fire safety design back to first principles.

This may involve computer modelling of evacuation and an analysis of the structure. This approach will also factor-in the risk of failure. (Will the fire detection, sprinklers, smoke control, fire doors, compartmentation, etc., work as intended?)

Means of escape and warning The safe evacuation of people from the building is paramount. It is expected there will be a large number of people in the building and should the fire occur on a lower floor, there will be occupants located above it.

It is common practice to adopt phased evacuation strategy in tall buildings, where the initial phase of evacuation is from the fire floor and the floor above. The following phases will be governed by the fire marshals' communication with the fire service.

A minimum of two protected stair cores are generally necessary for means of escape. The stair width is governed by the number of occupants expected to use them. Stairs need to be protected by a lobby to ensure they will remain usable during a fire event and provide places of relative safety for those evacuating, those awaiting assistance to evacuate and those approaching to combat the fire.

Potentially, lifts could also be used when a fire or blast has damaged the building. This requires robustness of the lift shaft construction, protection against fire and smoke, and back-up and continuity of electrical supplies to be considered in the design. Using lifts for evacuation can have benefits, as lifts can halve the evacuation time for a building of around 40 storeys.

Fire detection and alarms will be used to support the phased evacuation protocol for the building and will be managed to avoid overloading the stairs and allowing those not immediately threatened by the fire to remain in place and only be evacuated if it becomes necessary to do so.

Access and facilities for the fire service
To enable rescue from the higher levels of a tall building in relative safety, fire-fighting shafts are provided, consisting of a fire-fighting stair, fire-fighting lift, fire-fighting lobby, smoke control and a wet rising main.

Fire-fighting shafts need to be protected from smoke and the most common approach is for pressurisation systems to be adopted, although mechanical smoke shaft systems have become more common.

Active and passive measures for fire protection
Active and passive fire safety measures are implemented within the building to control the effect of fire on both the structure and the occupants of the building. Most of these measures are aimed at controlling the fire before it grows big enough to make a major impact.

Active fire protection
Apart from the need to provide smoke control to the fire-fighting shafts and to below ground levels which are being mechanically ventilated, there is generally no further requirement for smoke control on the upper floors. Smoke control could be introduced as part of the fire strategy should there be instances where travel distances are excessive and the time to safely reach the stairs needs to be increased.

Should an atrium be introduced, smoke control will become necessary to allow floors to be open to the atrium or separated by non fire-rated glazing.

The prime method of controlling a fire will be the provision of an automatic fire sprinkler system to suppress the fire at source and prevent fire spread beyond the room of fire origin. Sprinklers therefore support the means of escape from the building, support the fire service in their activities and also play a significant role in reducing periods of fire resistance if a structural fire analysis is undertaken.

In areas where the discharge of water is likely to cause a risk to life or be ineffective, gaseous suppression systems can be considered as an alternative to water-based systems.

Passive fire protection
Sometimes, the active measures put in place fail to control the fire and a severe (post-flashover) fire can ensue. The usual mitigation to this scenario is the provision of passive fire protection measures. This is normally prescriptively applied by ensuring that all structural elements have a certain standard of fire resistance under a standard testing procedure. In terms of a severe fire's impact on the structure of a building, the key functional requirements of any passive measures are to maintain the stability of the building for a reasonable time period to allow occupants to escape and to allow fire-fighters access to fight the fire.

For tall buildings, the impact of potential collapse has led to the development of performance-based design approaches to structural fire engineering which enable a better assessment of a structure's vulnerability to real fires.

It consists of an assessment of the most critical structural members in terms of overall building stability, consideration of the likely fire conditions in each area of the structure (design fires) and then determining the appropriate passive fire resistance measures to ensure that the building remains standing under those design fires. This normally results in a more cost-effective passive fire protection regime with greater certainty and understanding concerning the likely building performance in fire. This type of fire engineering should be carried out by an experienced specialist and should include complex analysis and scenario modelling.

Engineering

5

All tall buildings rely on engineering, whether it is to hold them up or to create the right environment for their occupants. Whether it is for the comfort, convenience or safety of the occupants, the engineering systems are fundamental components of a tall building which need to be integrated from the outset. Successful engineering should almost be unnoticed by the casual observer, unless of course they are contributing to the aesthetic of the building, in which case they should be expressed for all they are worth.

This chapter starts by describing the principles of high-rise structural engineering – including the additional considerations to bear in mind for megatall buildings. It then continues to discuss servicing and energy, the opportunities and reality of sustainability, and the critical issue of vertical movement and accessibility. Finally, we look at a range of measures that need to be considered for security – including how to design them into the building fabric and ensuring an ongoing management approach.

← *Hearst Tower, New York City*

Contributors

Kamran Moazami
Mark O'Connor
Ross Harvey
Joseph Burns
Nigel Clark
Meike Borchers
David Bownass
Alan Cronin
Chris Driver-
Williams

Structure and Stability
Kamran Moazami and Mark O'Connor

Structural layout and form The main engineering challenges of any commercial building are to:

- design a framing system that requires the least amount of construction material
- maximise the number of floors
- provide the maximum net-to-gross ratio possible.

From a structural engineering point of view, tall buildings can be easy to design but only if the engineer understands the critical issues and how they interact. The lateral bracing and the structural form of high-rise buildings play a major role in their viability, both in terms of cost and function. They need to be designed using optimum structural solutions; otherwise they do not become a reality.

The cost of a structure is about 15–20% of the overall construction cost but its efficiency and effectiveness affects every other component of the building. The financial viability of a tall building depends on maximising the efficiency of the floor plate. If items encroaching on the net area can be minimised in size, this is likely to improve overall efficiency. For example, shaving 25mm off the core walls and columns' diameters in a 60-storey building could generate 75 sqm of space. This is likely to have a value far higher than the cost of slightly stronger materials and the engineer's effort in maximising the economy of the design.

Tall buildings are essentially cantilevers out of the ground. As the number of floors increase, the gravitational weight increases, requiring stronger material for columns, shear walls and foundations. In addition, lateral wind loads and seismic forces increase rapidly with height.

A range of structural solutions exist to address lateral stability. At present, the most common high-rise structural forms available include:

- interior core (Figure 5.1)
- interior core with outriggers (Figure 5.2)
- perimeter tube (Figure 5.3)
- perimeter diagrid (Figure 5.4).

Some of the forms are only suitable and financially viable below a certain height. For example, interior core forms are usually designed by placing concrete shear walls or steel-braced frames around the main lift cores and service risers, forming a vertical spine to the building. As vertical transportation technology and effectiveness of service provision improve, the proportion of floor area required for services reduces with height. If the effectiveness of resisting a lateral force is dependent

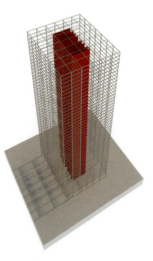

→ *Figure 5.1:*
Interior core

→ *Figure 5.2:*
Interior core with outriggers

→ *Figure 5.3:*
Perimeter tube

→ *Figure 5.4:*
Perimeter diagrid

on the width of the base of the stability system, then it can be that eventually the core alone becomes insufficient.

Such systems can be enhanced by the use of outriggers to engage perimeter vertical columns. Outrigger systems act almost like a skier who uses outstretched poles to provide extra stability. The poles effectively increase the base over which the lateral forces are dissipated (see Figure 5.5 for a simple diagram). The key components in outrigger systems are: firstly, the outriggers themselves because they have to transfer high shear forces and, secondly, the engaged perimeter columns which sometimes have to increase in area. Outrigger systems can sometimes be used in conjunction with belt trusses, which basically spread the loads across more members, increasing stiffness and keeping individual sizes smaller.

A disadvantage of outrigger systems is that they take up valuable floor space at particular levels. Perimeter forms, such as tubes and diagrids, have the advantage that they can carry the lateral loads on their own whilst freeing up the internal space. Perimeter forms work by carrying the wind loads in tension and compression on the outer faces and by shear on the side faces.

The diagrid can be a much more efficient perimeter form as it carries the shear loads predominantly as pure axial loads. The diagrid also removes the need for vertical columns, as the diagrid members carry both gravity and lateral loads. The opening photo to this chapter (p. 66) shows the diagrid structural system of the Hearst Tower in New York City. A disadvantage of the diagrid is that geometry and construction can become complex, time-consuming and costly.

Lateral stability assessment
Assessment of the performance of the different lateral stability systems can be undertaken by simple calculations at the feasibility stage of the project. However, as the design develops and the structure becomes more integrated with the other systems to be accommodated in the building, the assessment rapidly moves towards 3D computer modelling. This can be in the form of geometric parametric models for studying the finer detail of form through to finite element simulations of the stiffness and strength of the building. Figure 5.6 shows a full structural model of 22 Bishopsgate.

In terms of overall structural performance, there are a number of performance criteria that need to be met. The first is obviously strength; the overall strength of the system has to be sufficient to sustain the loads applied to it. The structure also has to be stiff enough that the façade providing the protective envelope of the building is watertight whilst undergoing the deflections imposed on the building by lateral forces. In addition, the structure has to ensure that the dynamic characteristics are such that occupants do not become uncomfortable by the inevitable motion set up when buffeted by fluctuating wind loads. Tall buildings also have to be robust under seismic, accidental and extreme events.

Floor system
Floor system selection is generally dictated by the column grid chosen. For shallow and modest span buildings, a concrete solution will typically prove most economical. For deep and long-span buildings, a steel (composite with concrete slab) solution would typically be considered, especially in the case of a commercial building. Figure 5.7 shows a model of a typical commercial floor design prior to fit-out. The steel framing system carries the weight of the floor and carries the loads into the column and core as illustrated by Figure 5.8. Figure 5.9 shows this floor system in reality, prior to concrete being poured onto the metal decking.

Figure 5.5: Improving lateral stability through the use of ski poles. The same principle can be applied to outrigger systems in tall buildings

Figure 5.6: Structural model of 22 Bishopsgate, London, including substructure and foundations

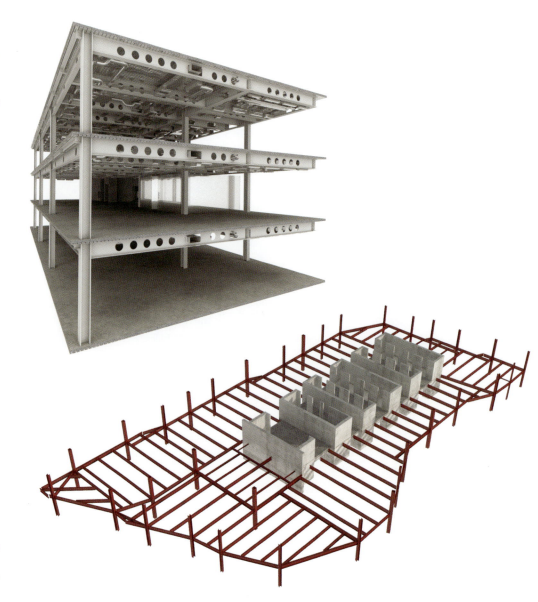

→ *Figure 5.7:*
Render of typical commercial composite floor system. The holes in the beams are for the services (HVAC, water mains, electrical, etc.)

↘ *Figure 5.8:*
Model of steel floor beams designed for 22 Bishopsgate, London

↓ *Figure 5.9*
Metal decking installed on floor beams at The Shard, London. A concrete slab was poured on the decking to form the floor structure

Design for extreme events

A key functional requirement which is becoming increasingly important is the design of the structure to perform satisfactorily during accidental and extreme events.

Globally, there is a requirement to design tall buildings against the risks of progressive collapse. Tall buildings are generally in the highest risk category for which a systematic assessment needs to be considered. Such events include design against earthquake, blast, fire and vehicle impact.

The attacks on the World Trade Center and subsequent terrorist attacks on other critical infrastructure have brought calls for tall buildings to withstand even more extreme events. However, such situations can place structural demands on buildings, which, if met by normal design processes, would lead to buildings which are functionally, economically and sustainably unviable. Therefore it is important to establish the key performance goals of the structure under each event and establish the necessary acceptance criteria that would ensure good structural performance in the most economic and pragmatic manner.

Tolerances and movement

Tall buildings exhibit particular movement and dimensional characteristics. The expected movements, together with the construction tolerances of the frame and floor system, is usually summarised in a Movement and Tolerances Document.

Differential axial deformation of the building caused by its own weight is also a significant factor and must be taken into account in the construction methodology. These small deformations must be carefully studied to ensure their effects are clearly understood and nullified during construction, as well as the life of the building.

Comfort criteria

As buildings become taller, the dynamic performance under wind can give rise to motion sickness issues. Occupants start to perceive motion at a peak acceleration level of only 5 milli g. To control acceleration levels to this extent would be very inefficient and uneconomic. As a result, acceptance criteria are set at the probability of a design event exceeding a certain level. For commercial buildings this is commonly set at 25 milli g peak acceleration under a 1-in-10 year wind event.

If acceleration is an issue, the main options to combat this are to fundamentally alter the dynamic characteristics (stiffness and mass) of the lateral stability system or to enhance the inherent damping of the structure. The former is normally prohibitively expensive, so enhancing damping is the normal choice. Supplementary damping can be provided by either a tuned mass, tuned slosh, tuned liquid column, distributed viscous or visco-elastic dampers. At 438m, 111 West 57th Street in New York City (Figure 5.12), is so slender that it requires an 800-tonne tuned mass damper to reduce sway.

↓ Figure 5.10:
111 West 57th Street, New York City, by JDS Development

Engineering 22 Bishopsgate
Ross Harvey

Figure 5.11:
22 Bishopsgate in context with the rest of the City of London

Figure 5.12:
The lateral stability system highlighted in red with the concrete core

A new tower at 22 Bishopsgate is a 62-storey office development in the City of London (see Figure 5.11). The building has a central concrete core, which provides the major stability; this contains the lift shafts and stairs.

The building is designed to have the following sway limits:

- overall sway deflection of the building, due to a 1-in-50 year wind, will be less than 500mm
- maximum sway deflection of any one storey, due to a 1-in-50 year wind, will be less than 10mm.

To achieve this efficiently, the building utilises two levels of steel outriggers, which have been coordinated with the plant floors to minimise impact on rentable space. The outriggers transfer the lateral wind forces into the perimeter columns, essentially giving the core a wider footprint (see Figure 5.12).

With the reduced sway, the core can be optimised to reduce the required concrete, maximising floor area whilst maintaining the required limits.

When they are constructed, the outriggers attract load, including the deadload and liveload from the floors above, as well as the intended wind load. This can dramatically increase the outrigger size and the complexity of the connection detail to the core. To mitigate this, the outriggers can be installed in the construction process but only activated using a locking connection at the appropriate time. It is important to balance outrigger locking against the cladding installation programme, which is usually the building component most sensitive to sway.

Substructure and foundations

The large concentrated loads generated by tall buildings ultimately need to be supported by the ground. The form of this support is also influenced by site constraints and the extent of basement space to be provided. Basement construction impacts the programme and is generally considered high-cost and low-value space – so this should be minimised in any scheme. Where deep basements are required, innovative techniques such as top-down construction can be used to minimise impact on the overall construction period, see more on top-down construction in Chapter 8, p. 112, under 'Foundations and substructure'.

Foundation solutions are dependent on geology. Common systems employed include piles, rafts and hybrid piled raft forms. Basement perimeter retaining walls are commonly constructed using secant piles or concrete diaphragm walls.

Figures 5.13 and 5.14 show exploded views of the substructure and foundations for 22 Bishopsgate.

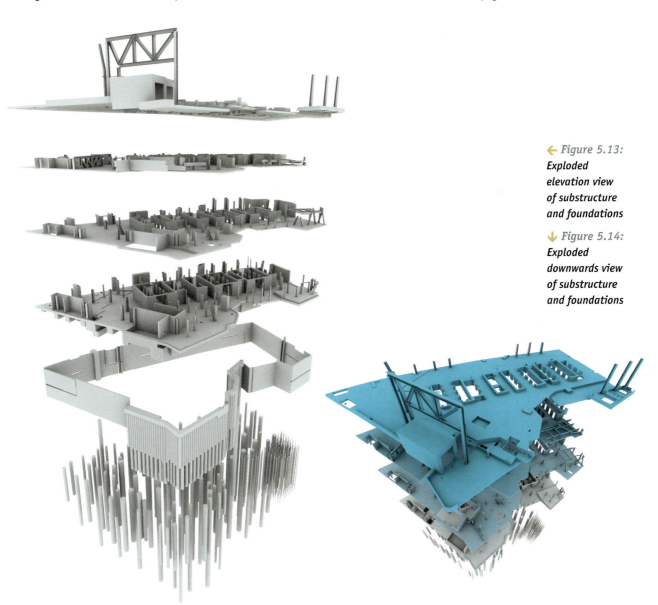

← *Figure 5.13:* **Exploded elevation view of substructure and foundations**

↓ *Figure 5.14:* **Exploded downwards view of substructure and foundations**

Megatall Towers | Joseph Burns

Megatall buildings are currently defined by the CTBUH as those reaching a height of 600m or higher. At the time of writing, there are four such towers: Burj Khalifa (828 m, 2010, Dubai), Shanghai Tower (632m, 2015, China), Mecca Royal Clock Tower (601 m, 2012, Saudi Arabia), and the Ping An Financial Center (600m, 2016, China). Several others, such as the 1km-tall Jeddah Tower in Jeddah, Saudi Arabia, designed by architects Adrian Smith and Gordon Gill (see Figures 5.15 and 5.16), are currently under construction or planning. As with all tall buildings, the most important drivers for the various engineering solutions to a particular building remain similar. For megatalls, however, the importance of these drivers becomes even more pronounced to the point that the structural demands on the architecture and planning usually become the critical factor in the success or failure of the project.

↓↘ Figures 5.15 and 5.16: Jeddah Tower, over 1,000m tall

Wind effects For megatall structures, wind effects determine the overall strength level but increasingly include the performance objectives of providing sufficient lateral stiffness and resistance to the perception of building motions (sway) by the occupants. A key consideration of wind effects involves the resistance to overturning, due to the combined effect of wind and gravity loads. Megatall towers such as the Burj Khalifa and Jeddah Tower have slenderness ratios exceeding 10:1. Extreme slenderness can result in overturning issues such as tension in foundations, extreme concentration of vertical load and other effects such as excessive sway or building motions. It is not unusual for such towers to require auxiliary devices that add to the inherent damping of the tower frame itself. Today, all such towers are exhaustively tested by scale models in a boundary layer wind tunnel; with wind loads and responses predicted for a wide range of storm events and wind directional angles (see Figure 5.17).

Structural materials and systems The choice of structural material and structural system organisation is very important to the eventual cost, efficiency and performance of the megatall tower upon completion and throughout its lifetime. Today, all megatall towers have at least some of the structural elements in high-strength reinforced concrete or hybrid steel/concrete compositions. Reinforced concrete is beneficial for megatall towers as it provides high stiffness with high mass (weight). The increased weight of concrete systems over structural steel systems increases the resistance to overturning and provides direct benefit in decreasing the motion perceived by the building occupants in wind events. The Jeddah Tower structural system is composed entirely of high-strength reinforced concrete walls and connecting (link) beams over doorways through the walls (see Figure 5.18). The system is uniquely suited for residential occupancy, as the wall system tends to create distinct chambers (rooms) between the wall segments. The walls are generally organised around the stair and elevator shafts, tenant corridors, and between units and partitions.

Of course, the structure of a tower – both tall and megatall – is only part of the story. The next section considers the special characteristics of servicing and energy consumption.

Figure 5.17:
Testing by the use of scale models in a boundary layer wind tunnel

Figure 5.18:
The Jeddah Tower structural system

- *250mm (10 inch) Flat Plate*
- *No spandrel beams*
- *9m (30 ft) between fin walls*

Servicing and Energy | Nigel Clark

Design decisions that impact on area or height are even more important in a tall building where loss of efficiency on one floor may be multiplied across all floors. An integrated approach involving all designers is critical to achieving the optimum solution.

The engineering services' design also need to reflect the proposed construction techniques to achieve speed of construction and to integrate with the programme's critical path.

An effective plant distribution strategy which achieves the optimum vertical distribution and which works in harmony with the architectural features of the building, such as the massing, façade treatment and vertical transportation systems, whilst achieving an efficient core with suitable flexibility to accommodate future tenant requirements, is key to a successful building.
For most engineering systems, a plant location serving approximately 15 floors in a single direction is considered optimum to achieve good distribution, good riser space efficiency and ease of commissioning, meaning that plant floors can be 30 storeys apart. For typical locations of centralised plant (see Figure 5.19).

↘ *Figure 5.19:*
Typical plant distribution strategies for varying heights of buildings

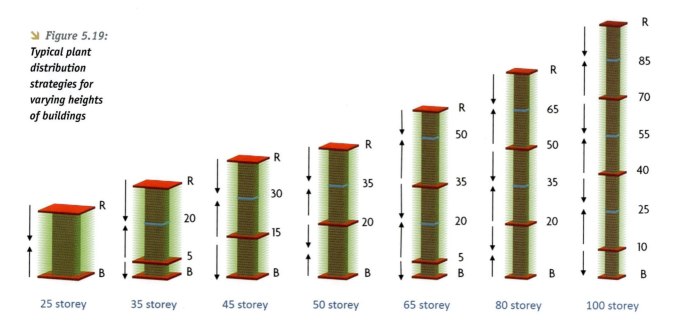

25 storey   35 storey   45 storey   50 storey   65 storey   80 storey   100 storey

It is often undesirable to locate significant ventilation plant in basements due to the impact on the public realm or concerns about pollution/extreme event, so a lower plant floor located between floors 2 and 6 is often a good solution. This solution was employed at 20 Fenchurch Street, in London (see Figure 5.20).

There may be pressure for intermediate plant floors to be achieved in a standard storey height to suit the architectural expression and rhythm of the façade. This can be achieved but is likely to require more floor area than an optimum height plant floor and requires more coordination with structure and plant replacement to ensure plant can be operated, maintained and replaced in a safe manner. 3D design work is invaluable in achieving this (see Figure 5.21 for BIM model).

The choice between centralised and distributed ventilation plant will have a significant impact on the core risers and the lettable areas. Service risers typically account for 17–20% of the total area of the core (see Figure 5.22), therefore strategies for reducing the riser area (such as distributed ventilation equipment) can yield significant benefits when multiplied by the number of storeys, but this needs to be carefully considered against any potential loss of flexibility for future tenant provision.

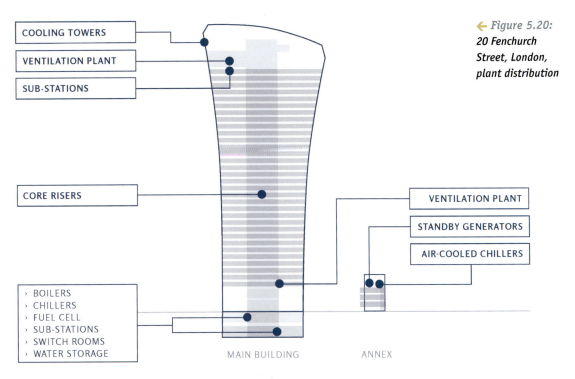

COOLING TOWERS

VENTILATION PLANT

SUB-STATIONS

CORE RISERS

VENTILATION PLANT

STANDBY GENERATORS

AIR-COOLED CHILLERS

› BOILERS
› CHILLERS
› FUEL CELL
› SUB-STATIONS
› SWITCH ROOMS
› WATER STORAGE

MAIN BUILDING   ANNEX

← *Figure 5.20:*
20 Fenchurch Street, London, plant distribution

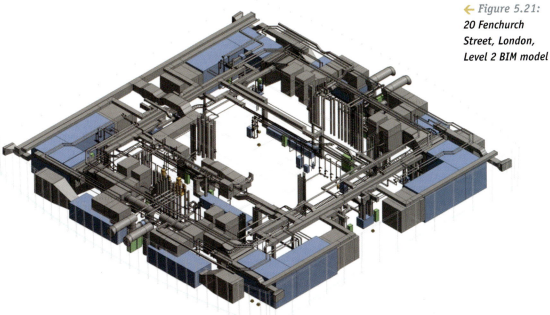

← *Figure 5.21:*
20 Fenchurch Street, London, Level 2 BIM model

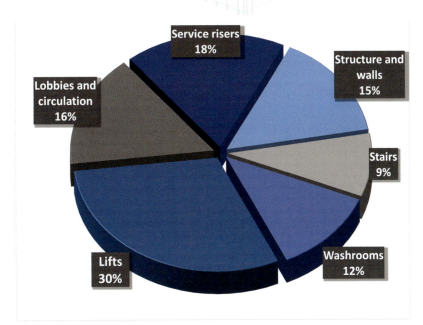

Service risers 18%

Structure and walls 15%

Lobbies and circulation 16%

Stairs 9%

Lifts 30%

Washrooms 12%

← *Figure 5.22:*
Typical core space use within a commercial office building

Because space is usually at a premium, water-based comfort control solutions are often used in favour of larger all-air solutions. Overhead solutions, such as fan coil units or chilled beams, generally require integration with the structural elements to optimise the storey heights. Underfloor solutions are used in some regions (particularly the Far East) and can be effective if combined with concrete structures, exposed soffits or minimal ceiling zones, and generally require less integration with the structural elements (see Figure 5.23).

Anticipating likely tenant requirements and having the capability to incorporate them into the building is important to attracting occupiers. This does not necessarily mean that the base building should incorporate these provisions as it risks an over-specified building where some features may

→ *Figure 5.23:*
Typical sections
for HVAC solutions

↘ *Figure 5.24:*
Anticipating
typical tenant
requirements

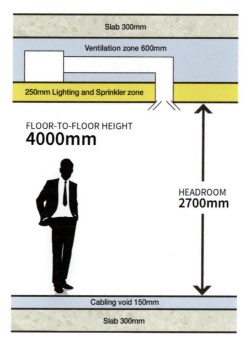

OVERHEAD HVAC

Slab 300mm

Ventilation zone 600mm

250mm Lighting and Sprinkler zone

FLOOR-TO-FLOOR HEIGHT
4000mm

HEADROOM
2700mm

Cabling void 150mm

Slab 300mm

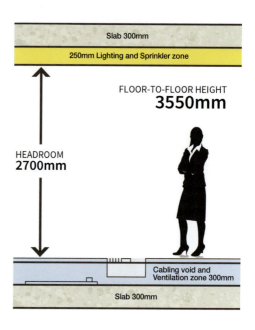

UNDERFLOOR HVAC

HEIGHT SAVING
IN EXCESS OF 10%

Slab 300mm

250mm Lighting and Sprinkler zone

FLOOR-TO-FLOOR HEIGHT
3550mm

HEADROOM
2700mm

Cabling void and
Ventilation zone 300mm

Slab 300mm

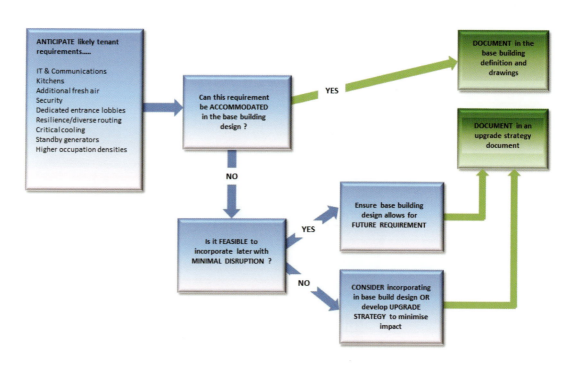

ANTICIPATE likely tenant requirements.....

IT & Communications
Kitchens
Additional fresh air
Security
Dedicated entrance lobbies
Resilience/diverse routing
Critical cooling
Standby generators
Higher occupation densities

Can this requirement be ACCOMMODATED in the base building design ?

YES → DOCUMENT in the base building definition and drawings

NO

Is it FEASIBLE to incorporate later with MINIMAL DISRUPTION ?

YES → Ensure base building design allows for FUTURE REQUIREMENT

NO → CONSIDER incorporating in base build design OR develop UPGRADE STRATEGY to minimise impact

DOCUMENT in an upgrade strategy document

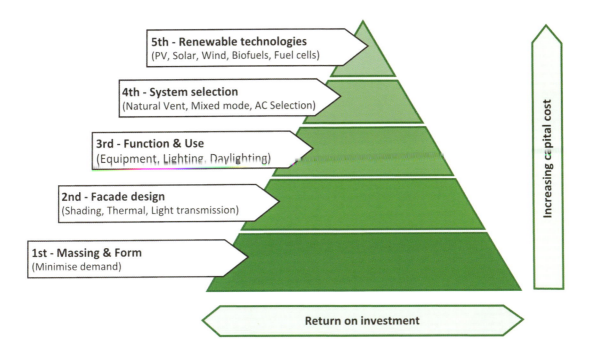

5th - Renewable technologies
(PV, Solar, Wind, Biofuels, Fuel cells)

4th - System selection
(Natural Vent, Mixed mode, AC Selection)

3rd - Function & Use
(Equipment, Lighting, Daylighting)

2nd - Facade design
(Shading, Thermal, Light transmission)

1st - Massing & Form
(Minimise demand)

Increasing capital cost

Return on investment

not ultimately be used. A more economic approach is for the design team to assess likely tenant requirements (see Figure 5.24) and produce an upgrade strategy document that explains how these will be provided if needed. This will be more economic and will encourage less waste, more sustainable construction and more energy efficient buildings in operation that respond to the demands placed upon them.

Replacement strategies for major engineering plant and equipment need to be developed and documented by the design team. Replacement of major plant can impact structural loadings and corridor dimensions in the design, so need to be considered early in the design development. With careful design, goods lifts can be used, limiting reliance on cranes and the resulting disruption to surrounding traffic from road closures.

Tall buildings result in a high demand for the land area they occupy, which will have a significant impact on the utility network that surrounds them. The market desire for electrical and communications resilience puts great emphasis on the integrity of the infrastructure. As the electrical infrastructure is under considerable pressure, particularly in London, it is common to take medium voltage electrical supplies at 22kV or 33kV, with the requirements of the supplier needing to be accommodated into the building design. Duplicate electrical supplies from different primary sources are also common for tenants requiring resilient infrastructure to support their business.

Adopting a robust energy hierarchy as part of the design process (see Figure 5.25), is even more relevant to tall buildings, where the larger façade area relative to floor area places greater importance on passive measures to reduce the energy consumption of the building.

Natural ventilation and mixed mode operation have been shown to be practical in tall buildings, provided that appropriate buffer zones are integrated into the building design (see Figure 5.26), to prevent wind gusts having an adverse effect on occupant comfort.

Tall buildings that incorporate a mix of uses also provide opportunities for more efficient energy design, by taking advantage of the differing load profiles and energy transfer between zones. This favours a more centralised approach to the main plant which could be arranged to ensure all users pay for the energy they actually consume, rather than on a pro rata area occupied basis.

Embodied energy should be evaluated wherever practical by the designers and the construction team, as should the sourcing and transportation of materials, to reduce the overall energy necessary to construct a tall building.

In the next section the wider topic of sustainability is discussed in more detail.

↑ *Figure 5.25:*
The energy hierarchy

↓ *Figure 5.26:*
The atriums or light wells are an essential component of the natural ventilation strategy at 30 St Mary Axe, London

Sustainability | Meike Borchers and David Bownass

The question of how to achieve sustainable tall buildings is not just one of making efficient use of resources such as materials, energy and water, but also of creating comfortable, durable, affordable and inclusive 'liveable' spaces.

→ *Figure 5.27:*
One World Trade Center, New York

A key challenge of tall buildings is often the loss of community spirit, due to the separating effect of floor plates and the lack of mixed use. Therefore one of the key aims beside low environmental impact construction and operation is to work towards creating a 'micro city', a vertical community that provides a high density of varying activities and enables an urban identity.

The prevalent separation through floor plates and a focus on rapid vertical transport into and out of the building often hinder social interaction of the building occupants and users. Current ideas about sustainable high-rise are based on a form and layout that encourage people to make use of spaces within the building and that provide access for leisure and mingling. Walking across floor plates and in-between floor plates is prioritised, creating a sense of 'neighbourhood' that also keeps people fit. Elaborate and well-placed landscaped spaces allow resting and relaxation within the vertical city or might even supply food in the form of 'farmscapers' [Vincent Callebaut Architectures, n.d.].

Building tall creates technical challenges for the construction and operation. To minimise environmental impacts and embodied energy requires close collaboration between the design disciplines and embracing innovative methods and products. Super-strength materials, such as ultra-high compressive strength self-compacting concrete and Niobium micro alloy in high strength steel, allow the use of smaller structural elements. This in turn generates more floor space and reduces the floor-to-floor height, a technique successfully applied at One World Trade Center in New York City (awaiting LEED certification) (see Figure 5.27).

Letting the structure be part of the architectural statement reduces the need for additional façade glass, as is well portrayed by the Hearst Tower's diagrid frame (LEED Gold certified design and construction) (see the opening image for this chapter on p. 66 and Figure 5.28).

BIM is a key component of super-integrated design and construction, as is the level of pre-fabrication. The LEGO style approach has found its way into tall buildings. Latest advances in this area led to a 57-storey tower in China being constructed in just 19 days and much higher towers of similar construction methods are already proposed [The Guardian, 30 April 2015]. The future will see these methods combined with other innovative technologies, such as 3-D printing and energy generating structural and façade elements, to arrive at super-efficient vertical cities.

Tried and tested materials and methods will also surely be part of the solution for building taller sustainably; however their capabilities will be further augmented and developed. For example, the still persistent perception that timber structures pose a higher fire and security risk will be overcome

↑ *Figure 5.28:*
Hearst Tower's diagrid frame, New York

soon. Good examples are the eight-storey Stadthaus timber tower in central London [Murray Grove, Waugh Thistleton Architects, n.d.] (see Figure 5.29), and the eight-storey Lifecycle Tower built to Passivhaus standard in Austria [Projects, Cree GmbH, n.d.]. Further 20-storey plus towers are planned in Sweden and Canada.

The basic environmental sustainability metrics of energy, water and carbon are readily addressable and managed through building taller. Heat loss through the façade is minimal, although cooling loads will generally increase as the impact of climate change becomes more established. Within residential developments, hot water demand is the key energy driver as population density is more dominant than space energy demand. Potable water is frequently minimised through grey water recycling, low loss fittings and a shift away from bathing towards showers. Ultimately, in the UK and other countries with existing low carbon grid electricity supplies, it is very probable that all the energy demands will be met electrically rather than through the current regulatory preference for distributed low temperature hot water (LTHW) and CHP use. In this environment it is probable that distributed heat pump technology will become the new norm.

↑ Figure 5.29:
Eight-storey
Stadthaus timber
tower in central
London

Environmental assessment systems BREEAM, LEED and other environmental assessment systems, such as QSAS and Estidama in the Middle East, all set energy targets that go beyond legislative requirements and require design to be carried out to specific industry best practice standards. Tall buildings potentially amplify constraints and need to test industry best practice to overcome them. Equally, tall buildings should also strive to take full advantage of any opportunities.

Examples of constraints: Tall buildings tend to have higher proportions of glass to exploit the views and are likely to be lighter structures, which can result in them having greater cooling loads, higher solar gain and more challenging thermal comfort.

Examples of opportunities: Better air quality and less external noise at higher levels present opportunities for façade integrated ventilation and cooling technology. High levels of natural day lighting on smaller floor plates reduce the reliance on artificial lighting and simultaneous demands makes energy transfer opportunities more attractive.

Tall buildings inevitably have a longer life expectancy than lower-rise buildings, so coordination and management related credits are more sensitive. BREEAM and LEED offer an all-encompassing management system which can help a tall building perform well throughout its life and are now recognised as adding value to lettable floors, both directly through reputation and indirectly through as-built quality.

As tall buildings are functioning more and more as vertical micro cities, the methods that we use to assess and quantify their sustainability is quite different from those currently available for individual buildings. The common metrics of energy use and water demand are of course still valid. However, as technology allows us to move to NET ZERO (carbon, water, waste) buildings, the metric of 'true' sustainability will focus on the socio-economic elements of durability, adaptability and affordability. Only time will tell whether tall buildings being constructed today and tomorrow will be sustainable, with future generations being the judges.

Vertical Transportation | Alan Cronin

Without effective vertical transportation systems, tall buildings are not viable. As well as passenger traffic, lifts are required for fire-fighting, movement of goods and possibly access to public spaces, cycles and plant replacement.

The size and number of lifts define the core layout, directly affecting the efficiency of the building. Too many lifts impact the economic investment but too few may impair the ability to lease parts of the building, so early specialist vertical transportation design input is essential.

Traffic in and around the building

Passenger lift performance Performance criteria similar to that described within the BCO Guide to Specification 2014, can be considered a must in the UK in terms of letting agents and for comparison with other tall buildings.

The assessment of passenger lift performance is made utilising simulation techniques with the gauges of performance being Average Waiting Time (AWT) and Average Time to Destination (ATTD)

The density of occupation considered at the design stage has a huge influence on the number of passenger lifts required to meet the targeted levels of performance. It is reasonable to consider different occupancy densities within the same building, particularly if the floor areas decrease towards the top of a building. Express zones extend the ATTD, although less than three intermediate stops should result in an acceptable passenger experience.

Arrival sequence and profiles It is imperative that the arrival sequence for residents and visitors to the building is clear and logical. Way finding and signage in conjunction with the lift controls is key to the ease of use.

It is also important to understand the occupant culture and location of the building and when the peak traffic conditions are likely to occur, as some building uses can result in intensive two-way traffic throughout the day (see Figure 5.30).

Control systems The control system is the way a passenger interacts with a lift system, which can be one of either conventional control where the passenger calls their destination within the lift car or destination control where the system allocates the call to the most appropriate lift, with passengers being grouped by like-destination.

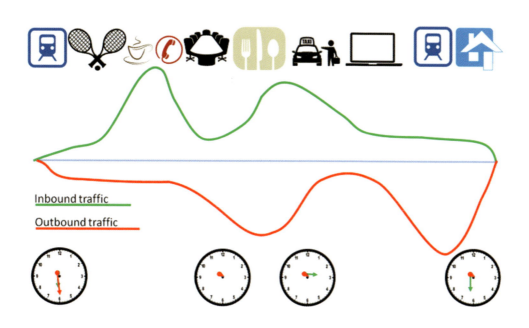

← Figure 5.30:
Typical traffic profiles for assessing lift performance

Inbound traffic

Outbound traffic

All control system solutions can be used within tall buildings, although the ability for the system to group passengers by their destination and reduce the number of intermediate stops to a minimum is generally well suited to tall buildings.

Core configuration
A single group of lifts has a maximum limit of typically around 14 to 16 floors it can reasonably serve. This introduces the concept of zoning a tall building, a separate group of lifts serving each building zone.

With a conventional stacked zone (see Figure 5.31) all lift journeys start at the main lobby. The building is subdivided into zones with each zone clearly identified at the main lobby.

Where taking all of the lifts to the ground floor is prohibitive, a series of zones can be stacked on top of one another with the upper series of zones accessed via shuttle lifts and a sky lobby (diagram). In mixed-use buildings this sky lobby approach provides a natural segregation between different uses. The Shard is an example of this approach.

Examples of how some tall buildings adopt these stacking arrangements are shown in Figures 5.32, 5.33 and 5.34.

Lift types
When designing a tall building, a number of different lift types need to be considered.

Passenger lifts
Single deck passenger lifts may be appropriate for transporting the number of people expected but for many tall buildings double deck lifts (with one lift car stacked on top of another) or twin lifts (where two lift cars in the same shaft operate independently of each other) may offer a more optimum solution. Since the advent of destination control, double deck and twin lifts are effective at moving large number of people very quickly. Currently the twin lift solution is available for only one manufacturer.

↓ *Figure 5.31:*
Stacking diagrams for single groups, stacked zones, sky lobby arrangements and up/down strategies

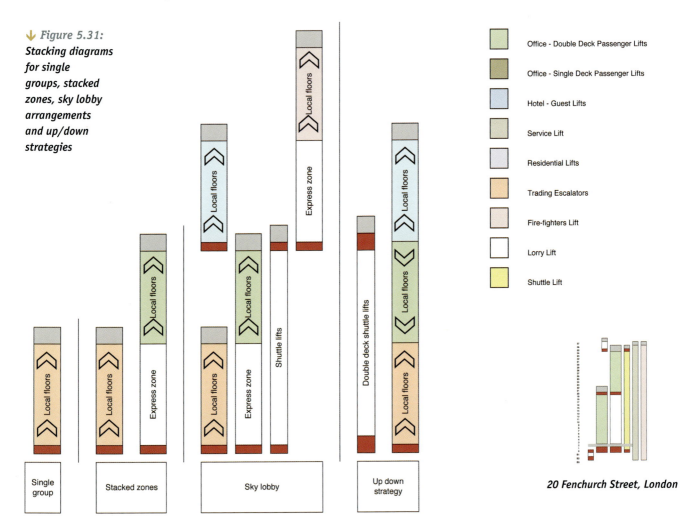

Office - Double Deck Passenger Lifts

Office - Single Deck Passenger Lifts

Hotel - Guest Lifts

Service Lift

Residential Lifts

Trading Escalators

Fire-fighters Lift

Lorry Lift

Shuttle Lift

Single group

Stacked zones

Sky lobby

Up down strategy

20 Fenchurch Street, London

Fire-fighters' lifts Fire-fighters' lifts are always required and need to serve all occupied floors. In the UK they must travel between the fire service access level and the topmost floor within 60 seconds.

Goods lifts The number, size and speed of a goods lift significantly impacts the ongoing operation and management of any building. At least one goods lift should be of an adequate size to readily accommodate office partitions and also form an integral part of the engineering plant replacement strategy.

Bicycle lifts New buildings frequently include space for a large number of bicycles, which are often located in basement areas. Bicycle lifts providing access from the bicycle parking area to the main lift lobby should be considered, as this removes the need for passenger lifts to serve beneath the main lobby level, which would adversely affect performance.

← ↙ Figures 5.32, 5.33, 5.34:
Stacking diagrams for 20 Fenchurch Street, London, Burj Khalifa, Dubai and ICC, Hong Kong

ENGINEERING 85

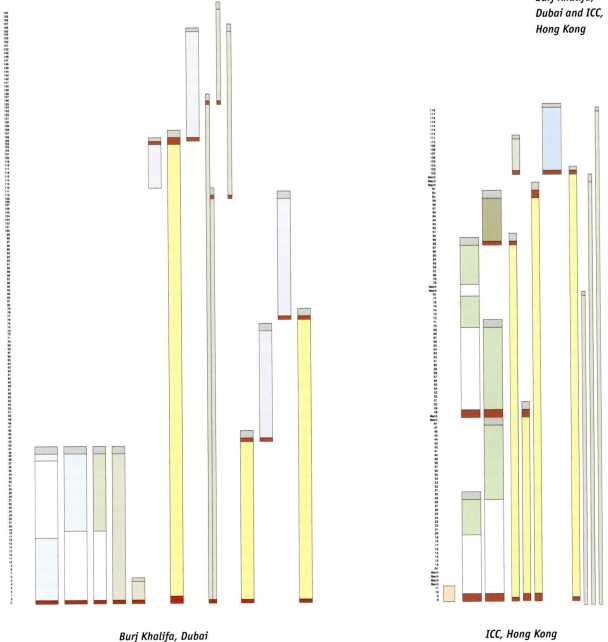

Burj Khalifa, Dubai

ICC, Hong Kong

Integration with security systems Securing access to and from the lift lobbies as part of a wider strategy is the most effective means of providing security. Integrating lift systems with the building security systems can simplify the arrival experience, ranging from simply requiring security clearance to the security system knowing the details of a passenger's destination floor. Integration with a turnstile provides a simple interface whereby the passenger has only one access card transaction from entering the building to arriving at their destination.

Ride quality Ride quality of lifts impacts the passenger experience and influences their impression of the lift systems and often the building itself.

The connection to structure and selection of certain system settings, such as acceleration (m/s²) and Jerk (m/s³), need to be set with Jerk being no more than 1.5 times the value of acceleration. Acceleration should be between 0.8m/s² to 1.0m/s².

Evacuation The use of lifts within tall buildings as part of the evacuation strategy is something that is typically precluded by local fire regulations, although increasingly there are examples where lifts do form part of evacuation strategies.

The Landmark Tower in Abu Dhabi was one of the first of a new series of towers typically twice the height of the existing tall buildings (see Figure 5.35). A gymnasium is located halfway up the building and the core configured to provide two independent fire compartments. In the event that the evacuation strategy is instigated, the low-rise lifts remain in service, picking up people from the refuge area (gym) and shuttling passengers to the ground floor. People therefore only walk half the height of the building in the event of an evacuation.

Using lifts when all of the building systems are fully operational can dramatically reduce the time taken to evacuate a building. Modes of operation whereby control features are invoked to address a catastrophic are even possible – for example, where the lifts do not serve the main entry levels in the event of an invasion or where lifts are stopped to prevent the spreading of toxic substances from a chemical attack are common.

Other considerations

Escalators Escalators are efficient people-moving machines. With a practical handling capacity of 4,500 per hour, they are often employed to provide access to amenity spaces, densely occupied levels and connections to local transport systems. Escalators are a necessary part of lobby and arrival sequence of a double deck lift strategy.

Mixed-use Mixed-use developments typically require separate entrances and vertical transportation strategies. Some efficiencies and shared lifts might be possible, but this is reliant on the ability to provide effective facility management. Planning the core layout so that local lifts within the different uses are stacked above each other should achieve an efficient core design.

Stack effect As buildings are becoming increasingly airtight, a stack effect can manifest itself at the lifts with whistling and sometimes landing doors being unable to close.

To mitigate these potential issues, door closers should have the ability to use greater force on closing the doors. The omission of ventilation within the shaft and minimising the potential path for air at rope openings also needs to be carefully considered.

Energy efficiency It is possible to achieve energy credits in various environmental assessment systems by incorporating Regenerative Drive Systems, LED lighting and switching lifts onto standby when idle. It is the case, however, that lifts consume a significant amount of energy in a high-rise building.

Developing technologies One major manufacturer has recently released their carbon fibre ultra rope. As well as overcoming certain physical restrictions, such as the maximum length that

Multi-car group with multiple exits

Local conventional lifts

Local conventional lifts

Local conventional lifts

Local conventional lifts

ENGINEERING **87**

can be manufactured and elastic stretch, the hugely reduced weight brings significant savings in mass. For a building over 400m in height, significant energy savings would result.

Another major manufacturer has released details of a rope-less system employing linear drives and having multiple cars within the same shaft. The system remains in development and currently has an anticipated availability in 2019. Such equipment could potentially be used in place of shuttle lifts in conjunction with conventional lifts, providing efficiencies in the overall area taken up by the vertical transportation systems (see Figure 5.36).

Security | Chris Driver-Williams

Cities have witnessed considerable change over the last 15 years, particularly in terms of densification and population growth. Tall buildings continue to develop and change, and communication methodology becomes increasingly elaborate. As a result, security provision options are rapidly evolving to address the ever-expanding range of tall building security threats – galvanised after the events of 9/11.

How does the security surrounding tall buildings differ? Criminals and terrorists employ a wide variety of tactics and strategies to achieve their aims, including antisocial behaviour, cyber-attack, fraud, theft, arson, assassination, roving gunmen and the use of Improvised Explosive Devices (IEDs). High-rise buildings are potentially vulnerable to all these forms of attack, but also present a number of special security concerns. The scale and high concentrations of inhabitants can slow down security responses and evacuations of occupants. Given the potentially large number of occupants, an offender may not stand out, making it easier for them to operate unobserved. Towers are often iconic, attracting significant media attention. The physical structure and location of a tall building and their resulting ease of access to the general public may also attract offenders. Finally, the fact that tall buildings are valuable assets, often with valuable contents, can result in significant financial losses following an attack or the theft of high-value property.

How threats can be evaluated and resolved A detailed threat and vulnerability assessment and risk analysis either via a classic risk-led methodology or by means of a more empirical 'Design Basis Threat' (DBT) approach will help the design team understand all potential criminal and terrorist threats facing a tall building and inform the design decisions required to mitigate them.

The risk-led approach follows a process of identification of threats and critical assets, assessment of asset vulnerability and calculation of risks to the development. This is a rigorous approach but any assessments must be predicated on currently available information; its use as a method of security risk mitigation only lasts as long as those assessments remain valid. By contrast, the DBT approach focuses on the principal means by which damage might be inflicted. Each DBT is then assessed for likelihood, based on variables such as the capability and resource needed to carry out a threat, and the recorded frequency of such attacks on similar developments. Once the principal threats are determined, the key vulnerabilities of a proposed development or intended occupants can be assessed. Design decisions can then be taken on incorporation of security measures into the development, whilst giving due consideration to the wider project requirements, such as cost and ease of operation.

Once the threats and risks have been established, protection of a tall building can be achieved by means of an effective deterrence-based security architecture through the extension and enhancement of classic security measures, such as physical protection methods, technical and procedural solutions.

→ *Figure 5.37:*
Threat levels are designed to give a broad indication of the likelihood of a terrorist attack. The level is set by the Joint Terrorism Analysis Centre and the Security Service (MI5)

CRITICAL	An attack is expected imminently
SEVERE	An attack is highly likely
SUBSTANTIAL	An attack is a strong possibility
MODERATE	An attack is possible but not likely
LOW	An attack is unlikely

Physical security methods provide a level of deterrence to a threat by means of physical barriers to delay and defeat physical attack. The design of buildings will determine the resilience level to the more obvious threats but will also influence approaches to issues, such as control of access and the protection of the development's critical assets. Physical security solutions typically might include:

- public address systems
- manned control room monitoring the site perimeter and public realm
- disguising, dispersal and/or duplication of essential facilities
- total segregation of activities, e.g. retail space from commercial space with consideration of shelter and escape routes for all activities
- perimeter security, e.g. vehicle barriers
- fabric of the building, e.g. enhanced structural design and blast-resistant glazing (see Figure 5.38).

Technical solutions provide the ability to monitor assets, detect unauthorised access, or identify and record suspicious activity. Such measures typically deter lesser threats but also provide the basis for a response to a more determined attack. Where systems are integrated with building management and IT-based operations, they can also be used as an audit trail for subsequent investigations and internal after-action reviews. Typical examples of technical solutions include:

- CCTV – internal and external including cameras, transmission links, processing, monitoring and recording
- Intruder Detection Systems (IDS) including sensors, alarms and monitoring
- Search equipment – personal, parcel or vehicle
- Automated Access Control Systems (AACS) – PIN, proximity or biometric readers supported by passes and identity cards.

↓ Figure 5.38:
One World Trade
Center in New York
features a blast
wall rising 55m
above ground

Procedural solutions aim to deter a threat by increasing the probability of detection and, where possible, are normally integrated with physical and technical solutions to ensure they are practical and mutually supportive. They may include searches, checks, surveys and inspections, and actions to be taken in the event of an attack. Crucially, to be truly effective, procedural solutions should include and be guided by a robust security management plan that ensures changes in threat and risk are tracked and new counter measures to emerging threats are developed.

Building operational strategies to minimise risk While
designs should always endeavour to incorporate future-proof 'smart-security' measures, such as integrated fire and security networks, forward planning and flexibility are key to countering developing threats and minimising risk. The key to effective operational security in a tall building is to regard it as a community. Developing programmes that engender engagement and cooperation among occupants will lead to increased surveillance and improved security awareness – an essential 'layer' of an organisation's response.

UK and international best practice In the UK and North America,
designing security into a building has become an established multidisciplinary effort involving the concerted buy-in of the client, architect, structural engineer, security professional and other design team members. Best results are achieved where stakeholders are cognisant of the need for security concerns to be balanced with many other design constraints such as accessibility, energy efficiency and aesthetics. Asia also provides good examples of best practice, as its building codes are often more stringent – even if it means using approaches that sacrifice rentable space. The 95-storey Shanghai World Financial Centre, designed by Kohn Pederson Fox, provides a fireproof refuge every 15 storeys to buy time for evacuees in an emergency.

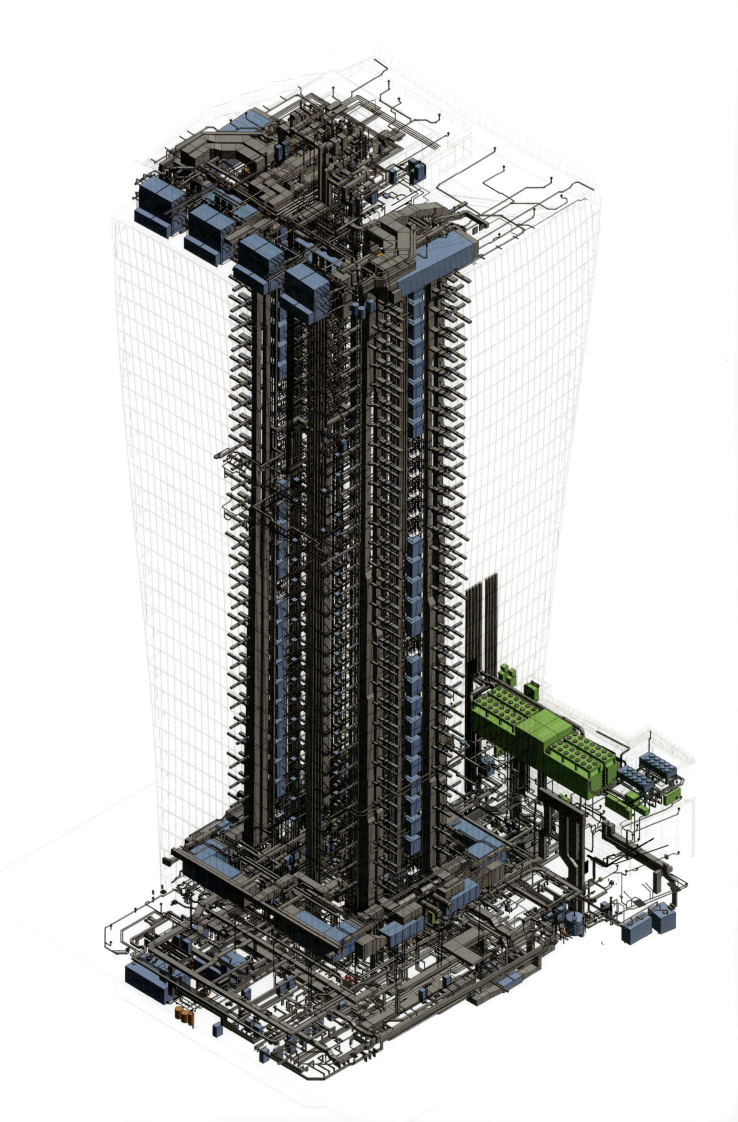

Building Information Modelling

6

Building Information Modelling (BIM) is transforming how buildings are designed, constructed and operated. It has the potential to add value across all phases of major construction projects, none more so than for tall buildings, where the benefit of a high degree of coordination and improved information exchange will be multiplied due to the repeating nature of building tall.

BIM has a direct impact on the way that projects are managed and on how construction should be procured. As BIM is more broadly adopted, it will fundamentally change how the profession will deliver services and offer value to clients. Occupiers are potentially the ultimate beneficiaries of the value created by BIM.

← *BIM model of 20 Fenchurch Street, London*

Contributors

James Pellatt
Frank McLeod

The Application and Value of BIM

The BIM environment is about asset information and how we all benefit from sharing and working with it. To enable this, the information must be structured and coordinated to allow it to be open to everyone and capable of being shared, referred to as Open Shareable Asset Information.

The BIM environment can transcribe the entire lifecycle of a facility from inception to disposal. However, it is often only found where individual organisations perceive value. To offer the maximum benefit it needs to start with the end in mind, therefore those environments driven by clients as end users tend to be the most successful.

This approach is particularly acute in tall buildings. Unlike other assets, they have particular challenges and characteristics, high investment costs, long gestation periods and potential for a high degree of repetition. The application of BIM technology can optimise designs, plan installation and de-risk project investment, providing a degree of predictability that allows development decisions to be made effectively.

In determining how to achieve the maximum benefit from working in the BIM environment, one should consider a series of stages:

- setting the environment
- in design
- in procurement
- in execution, and
- in use.

Setting the Environment

There is no single model that contains all of the asset information. It is a federation of many geometric and non-geometric models that are arranged to form a collective information model. This collective is hosted in a repository referred to as the Common Data Environment (CDE). The information is authored by a variety of parties, including Consultants and Specialist Suppliers, and it is essential that these inputs are managed through a set of project protocols.

It is important that this information environment is established as soon as is practical. The end user and project client must take a leading role in defining this environment and their requirements. This should start by establishing the Employer's Information Requirements (EIRs), which will define the said environment and the purpose of information modelling.

The environment consists of a Project Information Model (PIM) associated with the capital stage of an asset and an Asset Information Model (AIM) associated with the operational stage of an asset. The EIR must establish the clear requirements for the AIM and any client reporting or information drops from the PIM. These requirements should be programmed in a Master Information Delivery Plan (MIDP), which will show what data should be dropped from the model at specific stages.

The EIR will set the direction, allowing the delivery team to plan their works, which they will communicate through a BIM Execution Plan (BEP). The BEP is a live document and will define the purpose of the information model at each stage and will be reviewed as it passes through each stage to ensure it remains current. The BEP should be supported by a Model Protocol, defining the specifics of how the individual models will be constructed, and a Model Production and Delivery Table (MPDT), which will define who owns the information models, at any stage, and how they will develop its content.

BIM in the Design Stage

During the design stages information models can be used to appraise the potential designs and viability of tall buildings. The use of parametric models and complex analytics can explore the 'what if' scenarios of design developments. The use of structured and coordinated models, through adherence to agreed protocols, can allow models to be analysed and appraised, using specialist packages to understand many facets, such as: daylighting, wind, energy, carbon and cost. In addition, parametric models can be used to optimise components, such as those associated with the fabric of the building, particularly where the geometry is complex. There are some geometric designs that would prove very difficult to design without this technology.

Structured information can be used to explore the effectiveness of cores, net-to-gross ratios and the quality of the spaces provided (see Figures 6.1 and 6.2). As one explores the massing of a building's storey heights, internal areas and cores can change. Through the use of parametric modelling these variables can be considered in real-time as options are appraised.

It is generally accepted that at this stage the information model is considered as a Design Intent Model (DIM). The DIM is a geometric model with light attributes associated with its stated purpose. The geometry is developed enough to allow a robust technical integration to be proven, allowing the DIM to be used to prove the design, plan the implementation and trend costs through the design process.

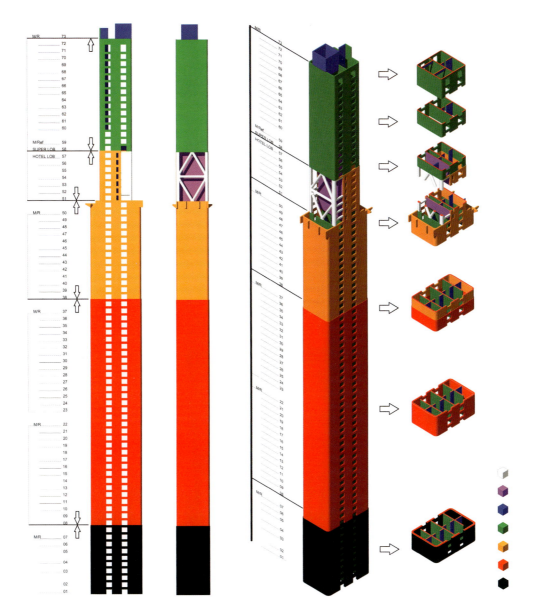

← Figures 6.1 and 6.2: (overleaf) Using structured and parametric information to explore effectiveness and efficiency

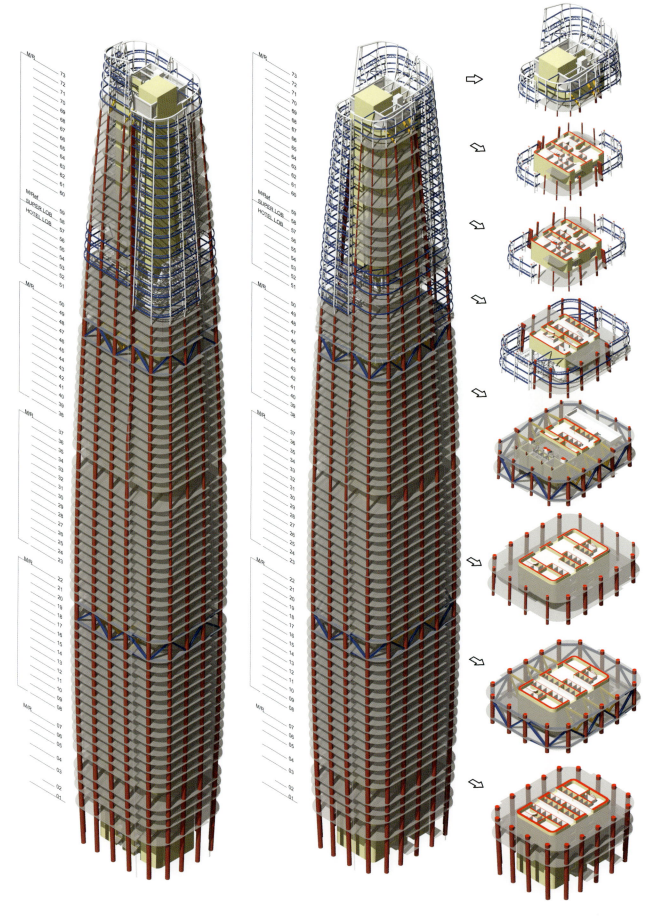

BIM in the Procurement Stage

The contractual language of a development is still generally two-dimensional, with the two-dimensional documentation being generated from the models. The DIM should be made available to the supply chain in order for them to understand, communicate and plan the execution of the works.

The use of a structured and coordinated DIM during construction can give greater clarity to the scope and degree of integration, significantly reducing both the supply chain and clients' risk and contingency allowances, enabling all parties to make informed decisions.

The use of basic asset definition and attributes can allow the early engagement of maintenance suppliers, leading to their early appointment resulting in a more efficient handover.

BIM in the Execution Stage

Over the last ten years, the City of London has seen a significant densification and the provision of tall buildings. It is not perceived that many of the innovative techniques associated with the delivery of these buildings have been directly attributable to working in a BIM environment but, notwithstanding this, the BIM environment has brought greater opportunities in the planning and communication of construction intent. Enhanced graphical techniques can be used to plan, test and communicate intent from a logistics, vehicular movement, deliveries, access, sequencing and individual lifts point of view. This ability can be used to virtually induct operatives onto the work site and plan activities extensively, which can lead to improved productivity and safety. With the potential for a high degree of repetition in tall buildings, it is possible to train installation teams in a virtual environment, particularly for fit-out activities, where early familiarisation can deliver productivity gains (see Figure 6.3).

During this stage the model develops from the DIM to a Virtual Construction Model (VCM). The VCM is richer than the DIM and is a federation of specialist supplier models, which systematically adopt or replace the components of the DIM. The VCM will have a greater degree of non-geometric information for the successful handover of the project and the transfer of the information into the AIM as an Asset Register Model (ARM).

The use of three-dimensional modelling has allowed off-site manufacture to be more rigorously explored, allowing digital virtual installations which remove risk and improve productivity (see Figure 6.4). This approach is not limited to off-site techniques and can also be applied to complex or repetitive activities.

The use of reality capture, through laser point clouds, can be used at many stages of a project to understand the reality and the context of a site. An area that is seeing a lot of increased activity, as the cost of reality capture reduces and the ability to manage large datasets increases, is the use of point clouds to understand the construction process and manage tolerances. This is particularly useful where there are complex geometric interfaces between packages or phases, where point clouds federated into the VCM can be used to validate the accuracy of an installed system and the ability for subsequent packages to proceed.

Digital snagging is now widely used, with the model and mobile technology used along with geo-positioning and the tagging of components on site to provide an efficient quality control regime where materials can be quickly identified and located, snags and remedial actions managed, and performance monitored.

This same tagging and the loading of the VCM with asset information is the preparation for an effective handover.

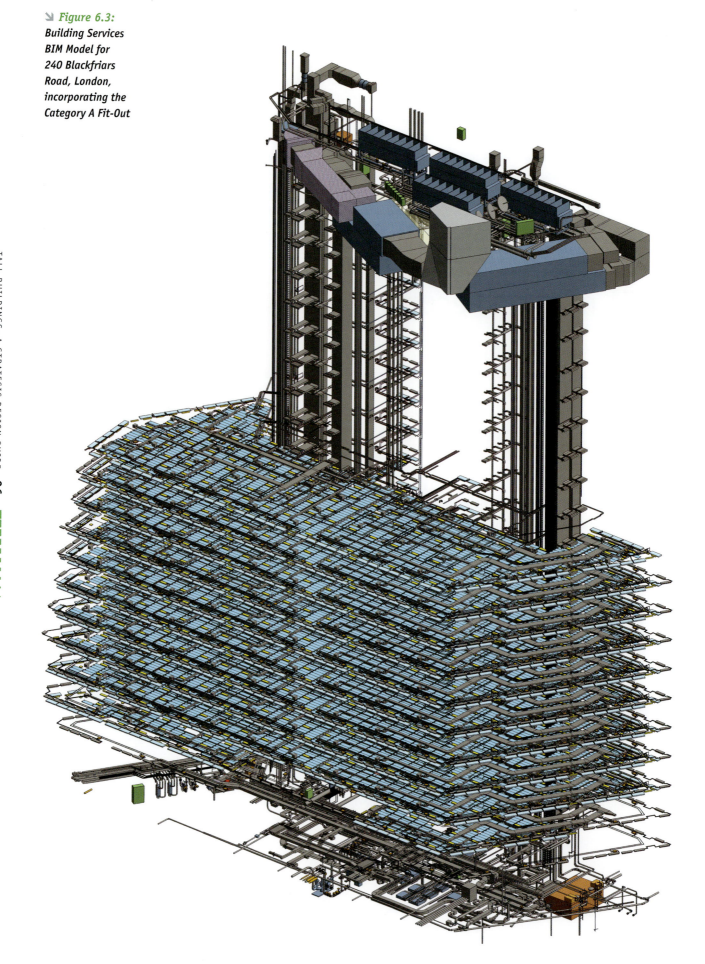

↘ *Figure 6.3:*
**Building Services
BIM Model for
240 Blackfriars
Road, London,
incorporating the
Category A Fit-Out**

REALITY

VIRTUAL

BIM for Buildings in Use

↑ Figure 6.4:
The progression
from a digital
environment to
reality illustrates
how risk can
be reduced on
the project

The application of information models in the use of an asset is the least developed of the phases of BIM. Although the benefits are known, they are yet to be fully released to the end user. The effort in maintaining and delivering information through the delivery stages often involves such effort that it does not present a significant return on investment. Where developments are achieving this, it is often the non-graphical information that constitutes the AIM. The geometric model or three-dimensional model is not seen as having a high value and the user interface is not as fluid or appropriate as the tools currently used in delivery.

Immediate benefits are seen in the adoption of an AIM, which are expressed by clients and end users as the early engagement of operational teams, the timely collation of an asset register and the availability of asset information. In the day-to-day operation and management of a building, the ability to track maintenance relative to a system or component can save time and money. Where faults are reported, the clarity of what is needed in terms of access, procedure and spare parts can literally halve the attendance times, with significant savings.

Funding and Cost

7

Height is not the sole criterion in the consideration of the relative cost of tall buildings. The size of the floor plate, the overall proportion of the building, its location and degree of architectural expression will all have a fundamental impact on construction cost.

Greater costs come during the operational life of the building and good design can have a significant impact on these operational costs. This chapter explores the cost metrics associated with tall buildings and the challenges of securing funding, procuring, constructing, managing and operating tall buildings.

← *One World Trade Center, New York City*

Contributors
Steve Watts
Yair Ginor
John Hannah
David Hodge

Cost Planning Metrics | Steve Watts

In the ten years since the first edition of this book was written, London has grown up in the high-rise world, completing a number of high-quality, high-profile towers. As this initial batch of tall buildings has negotiated the stringent town planning process in the capital, under the scrutiny of statutory bodies and the public at large, so the wide variety of experts in the high-rise property, design, construction and other spheres of consultancy have enjoyed the learning curve, now imparting their knowledge across the globe.

London has entered a new phase of tall building development. Further commercial office towers are in progress, along with many more residential and mixed-use towers. A lot of these are backed by international money, looking for a long-term investment in a vibrant and stable global city.

The fundamentals that underpin the commercial success of a tall building remain unaltered: cost (£/sqm), area efficiency (net: gross %) and speed (sqm/week) are the key performance indicators which make or break a tall building endeavour. These benchmarks exhibit a wide range of results, predominantly because towers come in all shapes and sizes (see Figure 7.1).

Commercial success will depend upon a combination of getting the big things right whilst addressing the detail. The shape (in both the horizontal and vertical planes) of the building is a more important commercial driver than mere height. The size of the floor plate, the regularity and repetition of the stack of floors and the articulation of the form will all have a profound effect upon these three overriding metrics, and thus the bottom-line (see Figure 7.2).

A key metric that represents the shape of the building, and which can have a dramatic commercial impact on tall buildings, is wall:floor ratio – that is the proportion of external walls for every unit of gross floor area. The product of wall:floor ratio and the quality (i.e. cost) of the façade markedly influences total construction cost (see Figure 7.3).

↓ Figure 7.1:
Cost versus height: a difficult correlation

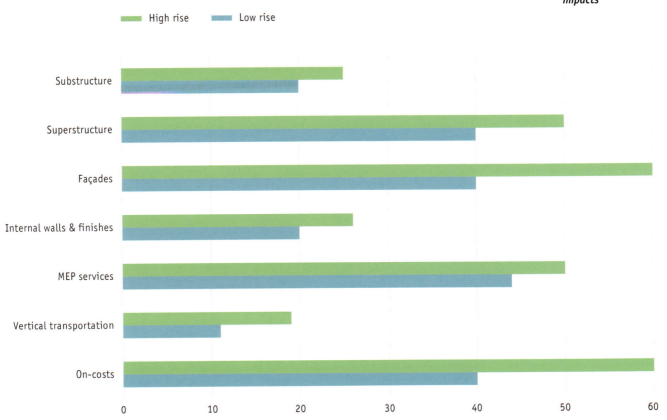

↓ *Figure 7.2:*
**From short to tall:
the elemental cost
impacts**

The table below represents indicative façade costs £/sq ft in comparison to wall to floor ratio (W:F). W:F is an efficiency measure and represents the ratio of external wall area to internal floor area. Typically a ratio of 0.46 provides an efficient and cost-effective model. If the ratio exceeds 0.46, a design review should test the design and value. The lower the ratio the more efficient the floor plate design is in relation to the external wall area and its associated cost.

↓ *Figure 7.3:*
**The commercial
impact of
wall:floor ratios
and façade cost**

Façade cost £/sqm									
	£ 650	£ 700	£ 750	£ 800	£ 850	£ 900	£ 950	£ 1,000	£ 1,050	£ 1,100
0.35	21	23	24	26	28	29	31	33	34	36
0.36	22	23	25	27	28	30	32	33	35	37
0.37	22	24	26	27	29	31	33	34	36	38
0.38	23	25	26	28	30	32	34	35	37	39
0.39	24	25	27	29	31	33	34	36	38	40
0.40	24	26	28	30	32	33	35	37	39	41
0.41	25	27	29	30	32	34	36	38	40	42
0.42	25	27	29	31	33	35	37	39	41	43
0.43	26	28	30	32	34	36	38	40	42	44
0.44	27	29	31	33	35	37	39	41	43	45
0.45	27	29	31	33	36	38	40	42	44	46
0.46	28	30	32	34	36	38	41	43	45	47
0.47	28	31	33	35	37	39	41	44	46	48
0.48	29	31	33	36	38	40	42	45	47	49
0.49	30	32	34	36	39	41	43	46	48	50
0.50	30	33	35	37	39	42	44	46	49	51
0.51	31	33	36	38	40	43	45	47	50	52
0.52	31	34	36	39	41	43	46	48	51	53
0.53	32	34	37	39	42	44	47	49	52	54
0.54	33	35	38	40	43	45	48	50	53	55
0.55	33	36	38	41	43	46	49	51	54	56

Wall:Floor ratio

Assuming the form is optimised at the outset, attention must turn to the detail, for significant improvements can be achieved through the aggregation of marginal gains. Honing components that are repeated thousands of times in the building can have a positive effect upon cost; conversely, making them complicated or difficult will have the opposite result.

A tall building is capable of creating an architectural and engineering statement and can yet be financially viable through attention at the macro and micro scales with form and detailing that allow cost-effectiveness, floor area efficiencies and ease of construction. From a supply chain's perspective, lowering the perceived risk will increase appetite for the project.

The impact of tall buildings extends beyond its site boundaries, and there are a number of factors that will influence the commercial metrics:

1 Location: including environmental concerns, planning constraints, site conditions and local practices and supply chains.
2 Scale: involving irreversible upfront commitments, significant early cash flows and limited choice of contractors/specialists.
3 Shape and detail must both be tested for impact, including economic.
4 Decisions must involve the entire design team to balance a wide range of concerns.
5 Understanding international requirements, including the needs of the financier, designer and local community.
6 Specialists are critical – in certain circumstances their input should be tested and peer reviewed.
7 Plan in advance, involving the contractors as early as possible.
8 Politics can be used as a means to make positive progress.

Are tall buildings more difficult to produce than their cousins? Yes. Are the potential rewards worth the additional risks? In most cases, yes!

Funding Sources | Yair Ginor

Funding a tall building is no different from funding any other major real estate project. When investors approach a prospective project they look at the total equity required, the risks and the returns on their investment; none of which is measured in metres.

With that in mind, there are nonetheless several attributes that tall buildings exhibit which impact on the way they are funded:

- they are large – both physically and in terms of capital required
- they take longer to build and to let, and cannot be phased – thereby increasing the timing risk
- by their very nature they stand out – for good or bad.

The resulting investment approach is not likely to aim for a quick gain, not rely on bank debt and not be contingent on a pre-let.

The following sections consider the equity sources and what potential investors are looking for, the issue of debt and the need or otherwise of a pre-let to secure the necessary funding.

Equity sources
Tall buildings are inevitably large and expensive. Even if bank debt were available, the equity required to develop a tower in London could be well over £500 million. So the question is: who has that sort of money?

One option is to share the cost and risk between a number of investors, forming a consortium. However, the larger the number of investors, the more difficult the management and decision-making is likely to be.

Whether as part of a club or on their own, there are a limited number of global investors that can commit such large sums to a single project. These are:

- sovereign wealth funds
- the biggest fund management businesses / life funds / pension funds
- a very small number of private investors.

Opportunity or Private Equity Funds are unlikely to fund the development of tall buildings, as these type of projects are unlikely to meet their required returns – usually 15–20% IRR (Internal Rate of Return) – but more importantly, they are unlikely to fit into the typical five- to seven-year life of such funds where the rigid investment horizon significantly increases the risk of a forced exit at the wrong time in the project's development or the market cycle.

What are investors looking for? Unlike developers or private-equity funds, long-term investors in commercial buildings are income stream-driven rather than focusing on realising a short-term gain through sale at completion.

To illustrate the point, consider a large pension fund that has £500 million to allocate and is looking to own an asset which will generate a steady, secure and growing income stream initially equal to or greater than 6% to match its liabilities – namely, making pension payments which rise with inflation or annuities (income yield is defined as the total income generated by an asset in one year divided by the total cost of acquiring, developing and holding the asset). If the market at present is pricing mature buildings based on yields of 4–5% then the only way for the fund to achieve the required yield over a period of ten years post-completion is by taking the risk of developing the building itself in order to create the investment and to convert the development profit into an income stream.

While the development phase is risky, once a tall building is completed it generally commands higher rents and re-lets more quickly compared to non-tall buildings in the same area. Tall buildings tend to be superior in terms of design and specification, offer great views and have a stronger presence in their local markets. The implication for investors is that tall buildings can better ride the typical boom-and-bust cycles of the property market and weather storms, thus offering investors a less volatile return over time.

Debt While bank debt can reduce the capital required and improve returns, it tends to be limited, costly, increase volatility of returns and comes with strings attached.

Cost is the first issue. When combining interest rates, fees and other payments (such as for guarantees), the total cost of debt may be more than the required return on the equity, resulting in depressed returns. This may not be the case if the investor has a 'relationship bank' that is willing to offer it more attractive terms on the back of long history, trust and, most probably, recourse to other borrower assets.

Secondly, banks will generally not lend more than 50% of cost and almost certainly insist on up to 50% of the space to have been pre-let (see below). This presents a very significant hurdle which needs to be overcome, not ideal when the un-let element of the space may need to be delivered in the bottom half of the supply cycle.

To pre-let or not to pre-let Investors, developers and lenders try to minimise development risk by pre-letting a portion of the building even before commencing the construction.

This, however, needs to be weighed against the risk of rising construction costs and the risk of missing the right time in the cycle. Even a significant pre-let will rarely be big enough to justify waiting, considering the cyclicality of the market, the long time it takes to deliver a tower and the fact that it is near impossible to predict market trends more than three to four years ahead.

Standing out Some investors may be attracted to tall buildings for non-economic reasons: as a way of making a statement or promoting a long-term brand strategy, which could be described as investing in 'psychological income'.

Tall commercial buildings are typically funded by large, long-term investors who develop an income-stream and are driven by long-term returns. They are attracted to the quality and relative stability offered by these type of projects (once completed) – and sometimes to the non-economic premium.

Having secured the funding and designed your tall building, it needs to be procured. Procurement will vary with the location and market, which is explored in the following section.

Procurement and the Market
John Hannah

There are three key drivers when procuring a tall building:

- time
- cost
- quality.

Limiting construction time is critical to securing a tenant and de-risking the development with tenants finding it difficult to commit beyond three years. The quality of the final product will impact the potential resale value. Therefore selecting the appropriate procurement process is a decision that will resonate throughout the lifetime of a building.

A key component is the understanding of market conditions and geographical influence. What might be preferred for one country may not necessary be appropriate in another. A simple example of this is the preference for Construction Management (CM) type contracts in North America. In stark comparison, Australia, the Middle East and Asia (MEA), along with the United Kingdom, all tend towards a JCT Design & Construct contract forms. Although the approach for using CM is fairly uncommon in the UK, it is still employed by some developers. The Shard, for example, was initially procured under a CM contract until it was ultimately negotiated as a fixed price solution.

Procurement strategies The desire for clients to obtain lowest cost with some cost certainty has led to the dominance of single-stage tendering. This has been traditionally accepted by contractors and subcontractors in stable markets with readily available delivery resources. However, from a contractor's perspective, this is only appealing for projects with construction durations of less than two years, with anything longer attracting greater commercial risk through inflation, with the developer bearing these costs in the original contract sum. In stronger markets, contractors will be more selective in their approach to bidding high-risk projects with long development and construction periods. In order to attract bidders, clients are often advised to procure projects on a two-stage appointment on an open-book basis and paying main contractors a fee for their professional services. This shares the risk between the developer and contractor, resulting in a potential for a reduced original contract sum.

There has been a significant shift from traditional single-stage tendering to this two-stage tender process in London as the market has picked up and inflation has resurfaced, with a number of tall towers in London (22 Bishopsgate, 100 Bishopsgate, Principal Place) having been procured via a two-stage approach. This procurement strategy is well suited for tall towers, allowing the design and early construction activities to overlap, thereby reducing the cost and overall development period.

Contractor involvement Whatever form of procurement is chosen, the early involvement of a main contractor can be invaluable. The ability to secure experienced resources and input into producing detailed logistics, programme, methodology and design elements in a manner they would intend to construct is paramount. This is particularly vital if complex engineered design solutions are required, such as at the 72-storey residential tower at The Address The BLVD in Dubai, where the contractor is using the world's biggest single jumpform to construct the concrete core. This innovative solution required significant technological inputs but has provided a significant saving in time whilst maintaining flexibility, allowing it to be adjusted as the structure changes vertically.

The engagement of competent specialist subcontractors, particularly in relation to the structure (steel/concrete), envelope, MEP services, lifts and fit-out works is vital. Each of these work packages requires a coordinated approach to design integration and prefabrication.

Regional variations The design must recognise the geographical and economic variances of a country and harness the availability of skilled subcontractor labour, plant and materials needed for the delivery phase. When considering the procurement of subcontractors, it is necessary to ensure that they have the relevant expertise and technical engineering skills. While this is no different to other construction projects, the main difference with tall tower subcontractors is the need for them to understand the challenges. Although there is a repetitive process of working on multiple floors, there is an ever-increasing risk when working at greater heights where their output and productivity can be significantly impacted by the weather influencing the logistics strategy.

In some regions there are very few companies that have the experience, resource or financial covenant to undertake projects of these size, so it is important to consider innovative payment models and vesting agreements to overcome such limitations. Through forward planning, design and increased engagement with contractors and subcontractors, such potential conflicts can be mitigated whereby each party is more likely to accept a greater degree of design responsibility and associated risk transfer.

Ultimately, success in procuring any tall buildings is only achieved through early engagement, teamwork and collaboration with the whole supply chain.

Post-Construction Ownership
David Hodge

Tall buildings by their very nature are considered prestigious accommodation, so a high standard of operation and maintenance are a prerequisite. The large scale of the operations can provide economies in scale but, conversely, the high standards in service attract a premium, with good communication and engagement between the building management team and the occupants within the building being essential to ensure the harmonious and efficient operation of the building.

Operation and access Operational issues need to be considered and integrated into the design during the design stages. There are significant benefits if the building management team can provide guidance to the designers so that the building can be operated and maintained efficiently with minimum disruption to the occupants.

As an example, One Canada Square, a 45-storey building in London's Docklands, has a Net Internal Area (NIA) of over 93,000 sqm. It is occupied by over 40 companies totalling more than 9,600 occupants with an average of 1,500 people visiting the building daily. The high density of occupancy represents just one of many challenges of operating a taller building.

The occupants and visitors need to access the building efficiently and securely, and get to their final destination quickly. A well-staffed and spacious reception area is more important in a tall

→ *Figure 7.4:*
Reception, One
Canada Square,
London

building (see Figure 7.4). The Docklands tower example has an entrance lobby of 1,500 sqm, with three permanently staffed reception desks and up to seven receptionists operating in shifts between 0700–1900hrs. Security presence is provided 24/7.

A failure of just one lift can cause major disruption to the arrival experience of the occupants and can place an additional burden on the building management team, so a high level of maintenance cover is needed to minimise disruption, often requiring a resident lift engineer. Due to the large number of lifts required in tall buildings, the comprehensive maintenance contract can account for 7–10% of the annual operational budget, compared to 2–4% for a lower-rise building.

Servicing and deliveries
A significant logistical impact on a tall building is the number of deliveries required and their distribution throughout the building. The Docklands example of One Canada Square has around 550 pre-booked deliveries per week via the loading bay, including the associated use of the goods lift. Logistics systems are increasingly sophisticated and can help maximise efficiency, whilst enhancing the security provisions within the building.

Postal deliveries also need to be well managed, with main postal services being delivered directly to each tenant, often with the part-time dedicated use of a goods lift for the postal service which needs to be taken into account in the daily operations of the building. Courier deliveries should ideally be at a separate entrance with scanning facilities to maintain security and prevent deliveries entering the building unchecked.

The handling of waste is a major task with the large volumes generated requiring regular collections. Typically, occupants sort and store waste for collection at night, which is taken to the compactors in the loading bay via the goods lifts. Cooperation of the occupants is essential to maximise segregation for recycling and minimise contamination, which would otherwise incur penalties for building operators.

Maintenance External cleaning and maintenance presents its own difficulties due to the height and large surface area to be maintained (see Figure 7.5). On very tall buildings the external cleaning can continue throughout the year, with interruptions from high winds, insurance inspections and any ongoing maintenance and remedial works.

↑ *Figure 7.5:*
External cleaning
on the roof of
One Canada
Square, London

The management team The amount of engineering plant is likely to be greater in a tall building due to the high specification, higher system pressures required and the number of floors involved. In-house knowledge gained by resident teams enables effectively planned preventative maintenance and improved response times. With a large number of diverse tenants being dependent on the building management team, the highest levels of maintenance are required. Greater numbers of tenants put additional onus on the building management team to provide high levels of control over tenants fit-outs, ensuring they do not have an adverse effect on the base building and ensuring records are kept up-to-date.

With the costs of operating a tall building during its life being 10 to 15 times the cost of constructing it, efficiencies and investment in operating tall buildings with complex systems and high demands on its infrastructure and building management team will not only enhance the reputation of the building to its occupiers but also provides a sound financial investment.

Cost is a fundamental factor which impacts every aspect of a tall building throughout its life, from its inception, through design, construction and operation. Ill-informed or poor decisions made at any point in the process can have very significant consequences that impact future costs over the life of the building.

Construction

8

Having achieved permission to build and having created a final design, there is the matter of construction. This chapter discusses the special nature of a tall project and highlights the ingenuity and creativity of the contractors capable of delivering such buildings. Leading contractors draw on international skills and techniques as well as completely new ideas aimed at speeding up construction in a safe environment and to a quality that is commensurate with the objectives of the product. The contractor must assemble, motivate and manage a very large workforce in a confined area, deliver thousands of tonnes of material to the 'coal face' at precisely the right time and ensure the safety of everyone on and around the site at all times. There is much to be learned from the specialist high-rise contractor and involving them during the design process is essential.

This chapter considers construction in three critical areas. Firstly, the unique methods and techniques are described. This is followed by a discussion on logistics, including lifting. Finally, the topic of high-rise construction safety is considered – both in terms of workforce safety and safety in design.

← *Principal Place, London*

Contributors

David Scott
David Elder
Gareth Lewis
Jonathan Inman

Methods, Techniques and Prefabrication | David Scott

High-rise construction is a complex task. It usually has a well-defined critical path through the programme, involving the construction of foundations, cores, surrounding structure and envelope. These, along with other ingredients such as the building services systems, lifts and fit-out, all proceed as early as realistically achievable.

In recent years there have been numerous developments in methods of construction, prefabrication and off-site working. These changes to the way tall buildings are built often revolve around improved safety, reduced programme and reduced costs, and are facilitated by technological improvements in the way tall buildings can be designed and planned.

Today's leading contractors use large, intelligent digital engineering models to plan, build and cost their buildings. These models often embed design and construction parameters, standards and calculations, creating huge data-rich integrated models which include everything from temporary works to cast-ins and pipe hangers. The models not only eliminate errors, avoid clashes and coordinate connections between prefabricated components but also, and increasingly, they are used to integrate the delivery, track the components, calculate resources, monitor the QA (quality assurance) checks, coordinate the manufacture, bill the client and even visualise the finished product.

Intelligent models facilitate virtual construction and allow contractors to better plan, test and develop alternative construction methodologies, before they come to site (see Figure 8.1). They can be used to plan methodologies, to train the workforce and to inform all stakeholders of all details about the construction process. They can be particularly important in liaising with the local community to explain rationale and activity on site.

↓ *Figure 8.1:*
Intelligent digital construction model of the Leadenhall Building, London

← ← *Figure 8.2:*
Full perimeter enclosure

← *Figure 8.3:*
Working at height in open conditions, workers wear a safety harness and are tethered to the building

Safety

Safety in tall building construction has been improving incrementally over the last few decades – see Figure 8.2 for an example of edge protection. Figure 8.3 shows a worker without edge protection tethered to the building.

However, working at height in exposed conditions is still dangerous. Improving safety has been one of the key drivers towards the growth in prefabrication. By using off-site manufacturing and modular components, work is moved away from an exposed high-rise building site to a controlled manufacturing environment.

For instance, it is becoming increasingly common for large prefabricated building service modules to be assembled off-site and placed into their final position before being connected to adjacent modules with minimal on-site effort. This is only possible through detailed digital engineering/BIM modelling. Figure 8.4 shows a 3.6m x 12m x 4.2m 18-tonne module from the Leadenhall Building that includes the main steel frame, the concrete floor diaphragm and the final building services.

↑ *Figure 8.4:*
Installation of an 18-tonne prefabricated module at the Leadenhall Building, London

Programmes

After safety, programme is usually the top site priority. Programme is determined through an integrated assessment of many factors and is heavily influenced by the required and available skilled workforce, permitted working hours, availability of digital models, space at ground level and the wind environment.

Uniformity and standardisation increase repetition, quality and therefore output. So it is important that the designers and contractor collaborate early, especially for tall towers, to inform choices between efficiency, complexity and standardisation. Floor step-backs, steps in walls, steps in column size and transfer structures are major design and construction issues that have a significant bearing on the construction programme.

Foundations and substructure

With tall buildings comes the need for large foundations (see Figure 8.5). The time taken for the construction of the piling, foundations and substructure for a tall tower can be as much as the time taken to build the superstructure; although it is normally in the range of a half to a third of the time.

It is not difficult to separate the foundation construction from the superstructure and some clients will look at taking advantage of the time to build the foundations and/or basement to complete the design of the superstructure. It is less common in the US, where clients will often wait for a complete design before approaching the market, in order to minimise risk.

Frequently, it is desirable to start the tower as early as possible before completion of the basement, or even before the start of the basement construction. A variety of top-down techniques can be used to get an early start on superstructure construction. Cheung Kong Centre in Hong Kong used large diameter shafts down to the rock to get the tower foundations built before exact tower height and width were even known. The Shard was unusually built up and down simultaneously from ground level, while sitting on steel plunge columns (see Figure 8.6).

→ *Figure 8.5:*
Principal Place foundation, London

↘ *Figure 8.6:*
Panorama of The Shard basement showing underside of core (level B2), plunge columns and piles (B3), London

Core construction Cores are often built using slipform or jumpform systems. Typically, a high-flow high-strength mix of concrete is used. Slipform is faster and runs at approximately 250mm per hour and is a continuous process. The speed means that it is less precise, more difficult to control and difficult to include complex detailing. Figure 8.7 shows The Shard, which was built using a slipform core.

← Figure 8.7:
Slipform core rising above floor structure

The main alternative to slipform is jumpform, which usually operates on a three- or four-day cycle. It is slower, allowing more time to check and inspect reinforcement and cast-ins before the form is closed.

Prefabrication of congested rebar, such as link beams, can often be very beneficial to construction speed but often need more crane time; this will be part of the contractors' cost/benefit analysis at an early stage.

Transfer structures and complex shapes
Transfer plates, transfer beams and transfer trusses have a major impact on building programmes, and the degree of complexity they bring to construction are often underestimated in pricing, programme and risk. While typical floor construction may progress at two to eight days a floor, a transfer slab can take much longer. With the International Finance Centre, Hong Kong, the transfer slab was designed so that the core could maintain a four-day cycle running through the transfer truss, and the truss itself was built off the critical path.

Steel and concrete columns
Steel columns for high-rise are often installed in double- or triple-stacked heights. Floor beams are installed from the level below with safe personnel access from deck-riders. Precast concrete columns are often a viable alternative to in situ as the reduction in crane time and programme will often off-set any potential additional cost.

There are many forms of composite columns. In composite concrete-filled steel tubes, the steel becomes the architectural element in a high-spec office building. There are also concrete encased steel sections. These composite solutions often take the best aspects of steel and concrete, such as fire capacity and fluidity to deliver overall programme advantage.

Floors
Metal deck on steel beams is the most conventional steel floor solution and would be typical in the UK for an office. Figure 8.8 shows the metal decking with rebar laid on top in preparation for concrete.

↓ *Figure 8.8:*
Metal floor decking

In-situ flat slab construction, with or without post tensioning (PT), is still the most conventional concrete floor solution but seldom used in the UK for offices.

As an alternative to conventional concrete floors, precast solutions can often reduce work on site and improve cycle times.

Digital engineering solutions are helping to create new floor solutions using precast concrete floors precisely connected to steel beams to create conventional composite beams. The 47-storey Leadenhall Building's floors were fully precast and installed by a team of five: three to place the units and two to grout the joints. Figure 8.9 shows a 3m x 9m megaplank being installed.

Pre-sets and tolerances
Provisions for axial shortening and pre-set are very important in high-rise construction. Since the movements are dependent on the time of loading, it is essential that the contractors and engineers understand and agree on the time of loading and the required pre-sets. With highly stressed columns close to lightly stressed cores, some of the floors may be super-elevated up to mitigate the effects of creep and cumulative shortening. It is particularly challenging where high stressed steel columns are next to lightly stressed concrete cores and it is essential to monitor levels and movements to adjust pre-sets based on their alignment with actual movements.

Future of construction
Large digital engineering models will continue to be the catalyst for innovation and invention in tall building construction. Modularisation and pre-assembly is evolving from creating large manufactured products in one discipline to the integration of products from multiple industries. This is leading to large pre-assembled products being built into tall buildings and increased interest in flat-pack buildings and modular construction.

There is no reason why a 60-storey building should take three years to build. If speed is a goal and clients are willing to commit to a team early, then there is enormous potential to build faster and safer than before. Specialist companies have shown what can be done through meticulous planning and preparation using a flat-pack solution.

Full modular construction is also developing and has now reached a height of 30 storeys; the technology and experience exists to go higher. With the demand for more accommodation and the reduction in skilled labour, it is not surprising that investment in modular construction is increasing.

The construction industry today is established around traditional companies that focus on a small part of it. The real opportunity is with integrated manufacture and delivery, and this will dominate the construction industry of the future.

The 'Method' issues described above are only achievable if the workforce and materials can be orchestrated and managed efficiently. The ingredients of logistics for high-rise are considered next.

↑ Figure 8.9:
Installation of
a 3m x 9m
prefabricated
megaplank in
the Leadenhall
Building, London

Logistics of Deliveries and Lifting
David Elder and Gareth Lewis

Construction logistics involves the detailed planning, organisation and implementation of a large complex operation. It includes:

- the collection, distribution and storage of materials
- the movement and welfare of personnel, and
- the removal of waste, surplus, damaged and unwanted materials.

The biggest contributing factors in determining the overall timescale of a high-rise building are its height and the floor construction cycle time. As construction progresses vertically, the delivery of labour and materials to the workface to maintain the cycle time gets increasingly challenging, particularly when combined with inclement weather, resulting in lost production. This loss of production can be predicted and the impact can be mitigated by implementing a well-developed logistics strategy. The principal areas to address include cranes, hoists and lifts. In addition, the issues around site management and the value of work with the design team are described.

↓ Figure 8.10:
Crane at Lexicon, London

↘ Figure 8.11:
Close-up of a crane at The Shard, London. The struts used to tie the crane to the tower core for stability can be seen

Tower cranes   High-rise buildings are inherently complex structures with varying floor plates, inclined or curved façades, and multiple terraces as floors reduce. A strategy that works for the lower levels may not provide the required service at higher levels, or may require extensive temporary works that are impractical or demand too much support from the permanent structure. It therefore has to adapt to construction progress, with cranes either 'self-climbing' or being relocated to a higher level (see Figure 8.10).

Self-climbing cranes and temporary support

Self-climbing is carried out with the use of a portable climbing attachment fixed to the crane mast. This attachment hydraulically jacks up sections above it, creating a space within the mast itself to allow the crane to insert additional sections, thus raising the working height of the crane. Where cranes have to be positioned adjacent to an inclined or curved elevation, the distance between the mast and the structure increases with the height of the building, leading to either impractical temporary works to restrain the crane or unachievable reaches. In this situation relocating the crane higher up the building should be considered, whether on a terrace, temporary platform or fixed to the side of the concrete core. Depending on the number of tower cranes, the climbing/relocation process can be a continuous activity rendering one crane constantly unavailable; this should be factored into the lifting analysis when developing the construction schedule. Figure 8.11 shows the crane at The Shard, which had to climb itself up the sloped façade.

Crane removal

On a high-rise building there will be multiple phases to the crane strategy. In situations where the floor plate reduces in size, the number of tower cranes required to construct the higher levels diminishes. As cranes become redundant, they are removed by the retained cranes until only one remains. It is the removal of this last crane that provides the final challenge in the crane strategy. On The Shard, the remaining tower crane disassembled itself to the lowest level possible (+240m) and was removed using a recovery crane positioned on a temporary platform that lowered the sections onto the street below; the recovery crane was then removed from site using the external goods hoist.

Vertical transportation

Hoists and lifts can provide an effective back-up when cranes are suspended during high winds, particularly on post tensioned concrete frame structures. Hoists positioned externally are still constrained by the same wind restrictions as cranes, however they may be shielded by the mass of the building so can still operate when cranes are suspended. External hoists typically have a large capacity for transporting cladding, pallets, medium prefabricated components and a large numbers of operatives (as shown in Figure 8.12). The main challenge can be the geometry of the building.

Internal hoists have a much lower capacity, usually positioned through temporary openings which can have an adverse impact on the construction schedule if left in place too long.

← Figure 8.12:
The red external hoist, used for delivering cladding, can be seen halfway up the building

'Jump lifts' Where a building core is constructed ahead of the main structure, such as with slipform construction, the possibility arises to advance the installations of the permanent lifts, albeit in a temporary condition, and this is known as 'jump lift' installation. Once a section of shaft is completed, a protection deck is installed, allowing the lift contractor to build a temporary work platform, lifting beam and temporary motor room – all within the shaft. Once the guides, electrical trunking and lift car are installed, a fully working lift is available for use by the main contractor. As the core progresses, the protection deck and working platform are raised and the lift serves more floors. These lifts are very fast, quiet and are not affected by weather conditions. They are ideal for the transportation of labour to the workface.

People and material management High-rise buildings, particularly those in city environments, require a disproportionate amount of labour and materials for the footprint of the development. With a reduced footprint and neighbouring buildings, access and egress from site can be very limited which, if not well planned, can stifle productivity. Prefabrication can often save considerable time on the construction schedule, and it also reduces both the number of deliveries and operatives, which can decrease demand on tower cranes and hoisting. Delivering workers and materials to the right place at the right time is crucial to maintain construction progress; however, to maximise productivity the location of office and welfare amenities need to be strategically placed to avoid excessive travelling time by operatives. As construction work progresses, satellite facilities should be provided near the active workfaces to minimise downtime and reduce unnecessary demand on vertical transportation.

Considerations for designers Early input from a contractor during the design stages can bring both cost and time benefits, as complex elements of the building can be assessed for ease of installation and safety. Local modifications – either permanent or temporary – can also be made to support the logistics strategy. Specific strengthening for crane ties, the temporary builder's shafts for concrete pump lines, temporary services and openings in the envelope or structure to facilitate hoists and jump lifts all need consideration.

Safety | Jonathan Inman

Safety is crucial in tall building projects; the complexities of construction are only amplified when working at great heights.

While the same health and safety standards should be applied on all construction projects, building high-rise is a complex task, with a well-defined critical path and distinctive features related not just to height but the challenges posed by the ratio of floor plate taken by shafts, the relatively large area of external cladding, the remote location of plant rooms and difficult vertical travel distances.

Much progress in improving safety performance in high-rise construction has been made in the UK since 2005 in a concerted effort by contractors, designers and clients. The ideas below capture a variety of issues ranging from legislation and construction of the superstructure through to practical points on innovation and behaviour.

Safety by design *The Code of practice for the design of buildings incorporating safe work at height*, BS 8560:2012, gives guidance to designers of tall buildings. It provides a hierarchy of work-at-height control measures that should be considered in design – these are equally applicable to construction stage planning:

The ability of the contractor to ensure that work at height is carried out safely is influenced by the design; throughout the design process design teams should aid and improve the buildability of their designs. Designers should ensure their designs are buildable. Designs that are buildable can improve safety by:

- *reducing the need for work at height*
- *reducing the time spent on work at height*
- *ensuring materials can be handled with the most appropriate equipment*
- *ensuring work can be carried out from a place of safely on the building without the need for additional access equipment.*

Standardisation and repetition simplifies installation of elements, increases familiarity with installation methods, allows for quick cycle times on floor-by-floor construction and reduces the exposure to working at height.

Incorporating pre-installed edge protection on perimeter steel beams, stairs and concrete slabs prior to arrival on site means floors will be safe to work on straight away, saving time and reducing leading edge working. Figure 8.13 shows the perimeter protection installed during the construction of The Shard.

← *Figure 8.13:*
The white fencing surrounds the entirety of the workfloor perimeters

↑ *Figure 8.14:*
Close-up of
triple-storey riser
module being
lowered into place

Prefabrication Prefabricated cladding units are recommended to optimise deliveries, handling and materials storage on site, and reduce the extent of external access required for installation. Specialist contractor experience in the design and installation of these prefabricated elements should be consulted before the design is finalised.

The design and construction planning of cleaning, maintenance and replacement strategies can greatly influence safety on a project. The opportunity for early installation of permanent access equipment can provide safe and reliable access system for completion of tasks at height.

There are various elements of building services that suit prefabrication, including risers, whole plant rooms or plant platforms. Service risers can contain multiple elements of plant and equipment.

An additional benefit that comes with prefabrication in high-rise buildings is that trades and activities can be more effectively split across multiple floors.

The key factor to incorporating any level of prefabrication into the building is allowing adequate time early in the design process to ensure full coordination with manufacture and construction planning.

Means of protection and access equipment
Working at height on tall buildings presents a significant risk to the public and adjacent businesses from falling objects, particularly in city centres. Safety screens are provided at the perimeter of the building just below the structural steelwork level and lifted as work progresses. All hand-held tools are tethered to workers to ensure they cannot be dropped. Every floor has full-height vertical fire-rated safety netting installed to the perimeter of the building as the structure progresses, guaranteeing that no loose materials can exit the building. Additionally, scaffold gantries and protection decks cover adjacent pavements and thoroughfares as necessary.

Wind speeds can increase significantly with height and special consideration is given to methodology when working at the top of tall buildings. Full edge perimeter protection will prevent most falls of material, but specific risk assessments and control measures dictate the use of lifting equipment and mobile access equipment. Height also sees an increase in wind chill and exposure factors, requiring specific awareness training, PPE (personal protective equipment) provision and work shift patterns.

Behavioural safety
Work on tall buildings in the UK since 2005 has fostered a very proactive approach to the identification and mitigation of health and safety risks, with extensive early dialogue between contractors and the Health and Safety Executive (HSE). The planning and construction of the Heron Tower (completed in 2011) was cited as an exemplar project by HSE in this respect.

Further, the adoption of a behavioural approach to health and safety management by major contractors in the UK over the past ten years has been particularly successful in the construction of tall buildings. Special measures for training, equipment selection, union representation, workforce communication and remote (high level) welfare facilities all contribute to a shared sense of ownership, respect and responsibility for what are often very high-profile projects. Figure 8.15 shows an example of workplace safety initiatives.

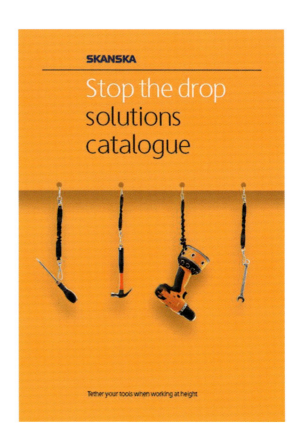

← *Figure 8.15:*
Example of active engagement and advice initiatives

End of Life of a Tall Building

9

It is logical to assume that a tall building will need to have a longer life than its lower rise counterparts, as the cost of demolition will be high and the practicalities will be challenging. There may be a reluctance to remove tall buildings that help define a city's skyline, so the ability to accommodate change and adaptation is fundamental to the good design of these structures.

Decisions regarding all life stages of a tall building should be assessed by considering the primary driver of their construction: the property market. In fact, 'skyscrapers should best be understood both as the locus of business and as businesses themselves' [Willis, 1995, p. 217]. Consequently, save for the few tall buildings that are owned by public institutions, commercial skyscrapers are primarily exploited to provide the greatest return on the significant investment made for their construction or acquisition.

This chapter explores the practicalities of legacy, change of use, adaptation or, where inevitable, demolition of tall buildings.

← *Demolition of Bluevale and Whitevale Towers, Glasgow*

Contributor

Dario Trabucco

Legacy

Tall buildings can become a distinctive element of a neighbourhood or a city. Their role as landmarks can grow over time, as they become prominent components of local culture. Their permanence in the city becomes safeguarded by local communities and preservation authorities after they acquire 'monumental' status. This applies not only to the building itself, but its branding and name are often elements of pride: the Willis Tower in Chicago is still called the 'Sears Tower' by Chicagoans many years after the name was officially changed.

↓ *Figure 9.1:*
Torre Galfa, Milan, vacant for over a decade

In many cases, the existence of a tall building is not critically questioned and it becomes a definitive part of the city's image. It is nevertheless interesting to examine when the legacy and permanence of a tall building conflicts with its ultimate objective: to produce a profit.

As operational costs (utilities, insurance, maintenance staff, etc.) are somewhat constant regardless of the number of tenants that occupy a building, it may be the case that rents are not sufficient to provide a profit. Utility costs, inadequate MEP services, and poor façade performance are the most commonly recurring complaints of tenants in old office buildings, and they represent a cause of diminishing market performance.

Examples can be found everywhere. When the 102m-tall Torre Galfa in Milan, Italy, was abandoned by its last tenant in 2006, it was the third-tallest building in the city. As of 2016 the building is still vacant despite its premium location and the success of several new towers built nearby (see Figure 9.1). When the final tenant was asked about their decision to vacate the building [Trabucco, 2013, pp. 38-43], they stated the reasons mentioned above, and also cited an outdated elevator system, excessively small floor plates, and a poor net-to-gross floor area.

Over time, as a consequence of a local or global shift in the property market, the functions tall buildings accommodate can experience a reduced demand. In this case 'extraordinary' actions are needed to update them in a way that responds to new market needs. In some cases, rents are unable to offset inherent maintenance and operation costs, and the most convenient option is to vacate the building and abandon it, sometimes for a significant period of time.

Change of Use and Adaptation

Whenever possible, the building should be adapted so as to meet the emerging needs of the market: these may be represented by a new function for the building (for instance, by providing apartments instead of office space) or to meet new standards of quality, services and appearance.

Re-use ranges between almost unnoticeable interior alterations to radical changes in the building's form, sometimes characterised by increases in volume or height. The extent of each intervention depends on the magnitude of the changes required to bring the building to its best value, though historic landmark status may significantly limit options.

A minimal approach was used for AMA Plaza in Chicago, where the lower portion of the 212m-tall office building designed by Mies van der Rohe in 1972 was transformed in 2013 into a luxury hotel (see Figure 9.2).

At the other end of the spectrum, the most radical example is probably the Tour Axa, in Paris, France (now called Tour First). The 159m-tall office tower designed in 1974 was completely stripped down and

← Figure 9.2:
**AMA Plaza,
Chicago**

↓ *Figures 9.3 and* ↘ *9.4:*

The extensive renovation of Tour AXA, Paris, shows a radical change in its interiors, external appearance and massing

transformed by Kohn Pedersen Fox Associates in 2011. The intervention was so significant that the final building was 72m taller than the original and is characterised by a more modern shape and a new curtain wall system (see Figures 9.3 and 9.4).

Many cases of office buildings being transformed into apartments or hotels can be found around the world, but the inverse transformation is not very common. This is predominantly due to the fact that it is easier to adapt an office building (more generous load capacity and floor-to-floor heights) to residential by subdividing the interiors with light partitions, than to do the opposite. Also, offices usually require more elevators than any other building function and it can be difficult to create the space for new elevators. The majority of high-rises approaching the end of their service lives are office buildings, so the transition from offices to other uses is not only more practical but also more likely.

In extreme cases, when feasible alterations to an existing building are not economically viable, demolition may become an option. However, this is a relatively rare occurrence for tall buildings, thus confirming that they are generally sound investments that can provide profits for a very long time.

In fact, despite the fact that there are now globally more than 3,400 towers exceeding 150m in height, only four such buildings have been voluntarily demolished in the past (see Figure 9.5).

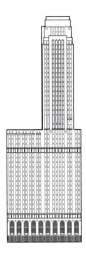

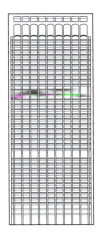

SINGER BUILDING

New York
187m high
Built in 1908
Demolished in 1968

Obsolescence – new bigger building built on site

MORRISON HOTEL

Chicago
160m high
Built in 1925
Demolished in 1965

Obsolescence – new bigger building with another function built on site

DEUTSCHE BANK

New York
158m high
Built in 1974
Demolished in 2011

Damages suffered during the 9/11, 2001 attack on New York City (see Figure 9.6)

ONE MERIDIAN PLAZA

Philadelphia
150m high
Built in 1972
Demolished in 1999

Damages suffered during a fire

↑ *Figure 9.5:*
Tallest demolished buildings

← *Figure 9.6:*
Deutsche Bank building damages, New York

Demolition

The remarkable discrepancy between the number of existing 150m-plus buildings and the number of those that have been demolished unveils an important problem: developers around the world are now building structures six times taller (and many more times bulkier) than the industry is capable of demolishing, thus potentially underestimating the impact that the ageing tall building stock will have in the future.

Three major demolition contractors from the US, Europe and Japan volunteered to undertake a theoretical research project. This exercise considered the demolition of a hypothetical 60-storey building located in central Chicago. The results of this study evidenced the emergence of a problem: using current demolition technologies, the deconstruction of the hypothetical tower would require approximately 30 to 36 months. This is considerable, especially when compared to the 18–24 months' construction time of such a tower. During this period, noise, dust and vibrations would be continuously disruptive for neighbouring buildings. The whole city would suffer from the traffic generated by the trucks required to remove the building's materials, which is calculated to be between 40,000 and 130,000 tonnes of debris (for structural elements only). Figure 9.7 shows how hoisting equipment is used in demolition. Small- and medium-sized equipment are hoisted on the building roof to start the process. The floor-bearing capacity and the ability to move among structural elements limit the possibility to use larger equipment and, consequently, slows down the demolition activities.

However, evidence suggests that this will become a more common occurrence, as many towers built after the Second World War are now approaching the end of their service lives. Demolition can also be required as a consequence of a catastrophic event, such as an uncontrolled fire, major earthquake or terrorist attack.

↑ *Figure 9.7*
Hoisting equipment used in demolition

The idea that tall buildings can be demolished through a controlled collapse using explosives or the weakening of certain structural elements is quite popular. When tall buildings are not located in a dense urban environment, this is indeed a possibility. The demolition work (carried out by Reisch Sprengtechnik) on the 116m-tall concrete AfE Turm in Frankfurt is, so far, the tallest building demolished with explosives.

This solution, which might seem faster than other methods, actually requires a lot of time and preparation, as a careful analysis of the structural elements of the building needs to be performed in order to calculate the amount and positions of explosives. Despite being extensively used in the US for the demolition of several buildings in compact urban areas, liabilities for the surrounding buildings, potential damages to underground infrastructure, and the dust and vibrations provoked by the collapsing building suggest that this system is not applicable to densely-located tall buildings.

None of the four tallest demolition projects featured in Figure 9.5 employed a controlled collapse. A slow deconstruction process was used in these cases, where small excavators and cranes were used to transfer demolition debris to the ground. Several technologies are now being developed to facilitate this method and to avoid the construction of scaffolds entirely around the structure.

In 2015, the Italian contractor Despe demolished two residential towers in Glasgow with a proprietary method consisting of a scaffolding 'hat' built on top of the tower to contain the demolition work, preventing falling debris and the propagation of dust and noise. The three-storey 'hat' descends via hydraulic jacks as the demolition process moves from top to bottom.

A similar system is being used by a Japanese contractor, Taisei. In this case, the actual roof of the building is maintained to protect the demolition works happening within a scaffolding 'hat' which imitates the building façade. This is progressively lowered as demolition proceeds to prevent the spread of noise and dust [Kayashima et al, 2012, pp. 631-36]. This system has been used for the demolition of various buildings in the past few years, with the largest application being the Grand Prince Hotel Akasaka, a 39-storey tower in Tokyo that was unable to be updated given its excessively low ceilings (see Figures 9.8–9.11).

Another Japanese methodology calls for the entire building to be supported by hydraulic jacks while columns on the ground floor are being cut, making it seem as though it is disappearing under the ground [Mizutani and Yoshikai, 2011, pp. 36-41]. When the entire ground floor structure is demolished, the building is lowered down by the jacks and the process starts again. This solution requires a temporary steel bracing system to be constructed around the core of the tower in order to stabilise the building in the event of an earthquake. Since the demolition process takes place at ground level, demolition tools and debris are easily transported and the spread of noise and dust is limited. Conventional demolition systems require the construction of a scaffolding structure all around the building. The hoisting of heavy equipment and the demolishing operations happen on the roof, thus facilitating the diffusion of noise and dust. With the demolition system invented by Kajima, the demolition happens at the ground level, propagating all operations (see Figures 9.12–9.15).

Office buildings, as everything, are often optimised to serve a single function. However, this may lead to a premature need to modify the building should the demand change. Alternatively, a building can be designed to be as flexible and adaptable as possible, but this may lead to a more expensive building, as it may have to accommodate elements that are not needed for the initial function. Developers, clients and designers must strive to find the right balance between specific needs and adaptability to create long-term sustainable and economic solutions.

↓ Figures 9.8, 9.9, 9.10 and 9.11: **Demolition sequence of the Grand Prince Hotel Akasaka, Tokyo**

↓↓ Figures 9.12, 9.13, 9.14 and 9.15: **Demolition sequence of the Kajima Headquarters, Tokyo**

The Next Generation

10

In London, the period 2005–15 delivered a significant change to the skyline. A similar change occurred in many other cities around the world, although few have London's historic significance and the strict controls exerted by its planning system. As the world population increases and cities become denser, we will see changing skylines, new building forms and improved transport and working practices. This chapter looks to the future of high-rise in different kinds of cities and what might be the drivers affecting new generations of tall buildings.

← *The Interlace, Singapore*

Contributor
Dr Antony Wood

Tomorrow's Skyscrapers

Despite notable advances in the quality of construction, materials and technology, the typical skyscraper has not changed much from the predominant glass-and-steel aesthetic championed by Modernism in the 1950s. The rectilinear, air-conditioned, glass-skinned box is still the main template for the majority of tall buildings being developed around the world.

A smaller group of ever-more adventurous sculptural forms have come to the forefront alongside the more commercially inclined boxes over the past decade or two. In both the 'box' and the 'sculptural' approach, the relationship between the building and its location is predominantly commercial or visual. These buildings are largely divorced from the specifics of the place they inhabit – physically, culturally, environmentally and, often, socially too. For hundreds, even thousands, of years the vernacular architecture in many of the locations that now host tall buildings had to be intrinsically tied into its location – for its materials, its ventilation and its ability to function within a given climate and culture. Modernism rejected all this in the belief of a 'universal architecture', which transcended mere 'context' and worked on a higher philosophical plane.

The consequence of this was the aesthetic and cultural homogenisation of cities around the world – a force that has gathered pace exponentially over the past two decades, with today's easier flow of capital, labour, goods and architectural models. Now a 'progressive' city is largely defined by its set of skyscraper icons, but the association is largely synonymous rather than indigenous – the same set of icons would become as well identified with other cities in the world if they were placed there (see Figure 10.1). The models are thus readily transportable.

Of course it is difficult to talk about 'indigenousness' in a building type that has only 130 years of history, and which has now spread from its North American roots to encompass almost the entire world. Both the words 'indigenous' and 'vernacular' imply a long-standing connection with a culture, so how can a relative newcomer even be considered in such terms? The answer, of course, is that we need to consider the future, and how the tall buildings being built today will reflect their culture and setting in 100 or 200 years from now. After all, many of them will still be around for that time; the industry has yet to constructively dismantle/demolish a building over 200m in height, let alone the 1,000m heights we are starting to see today. Thus, the buildings we are realising today will become the vernacular of a place tomorrow – a huge responsibility.

This chapter outlines ten design principles that would result in tall buildings being more related to their locations. It articulates a locally specific approach to skyscrapers and uses built examples to illustrate the points made. These principles are not intended to be approached in isolation. Perhaps the very best buildings would embrace all principles, though some might not be possible in certain locales. Ultimately, the intention is to inspire a regionalist [Powell, 1993] approach to tall building design, where skyscrapers in Shanghai function every bit as well as those in Seattle or Sydney in commercial and energy terms, but feel as if they are a part of a local vernacular, a local response.

→ *Figure 10.1: Interchangeable panoramas, from top to bottom: Warsaw, Miami, Melbourne and Manila*

Design Principles

1. Tall buildings should relate to the physical characteristics of place

Virtually all cities have an existing physical legacy, an 'evident built infrastructure' – streets, spaces, urban axes, buildings, monuments, other objects. The tall building – though potentially dwarfing many of these existing elements in scale – should respect and physically embrace this existing 'urban grain' by extending circulation routes into and through the site. This approach would allow important nearby monuments and viewing corridors to impact the form or expression of the building. An example of this is the sloping form of the Leadenhall Building, London, which came about so as not to block the views to St Paul's Cathedral and the existing Grade 1-listed St Andrew Undershaft church to the east of the site (see Figure 10.2).

2. Tall buildings should relate to the environmental characteristics of place

This is considered perhaps the most important aspect of creating sustainable tall buildings, which the Modernist universal architecture most disdained. For any building to truly be environmental, it needs to not only respect all aspects of local climate, but it must maximise the potential for using each aspect of climate within the building. Not only should sun, light, wind, air and rain have as minimal a negative effect as possible on the building, but it should also be embraced into the building. Wind and air buoyancy should be used for natural ventilation so that tall buildings, irrespective of building function, could be naturally ventilated for at least part of the period needed. Solar panels have occasionally been embraced but there are perhaps greater returns from incorporating technologies such as solar-thermal systems into the skin of a skyscraper (especially in intense solar environments) or using solar energy capture for phase-change materials.

Much of the tall building world thought wind harvesting was the technology with the greatest potential for generating energy in skyscrapers a decade or so ago, and yet to date we see only three tall buildings with significant wind turbines: Bahrain World Trade Center, 2008; Strata Building, London, 2010; and Pearl River Tower, Guangzhou, China, 2012 (see Figure 10.3). At least two of these have reported considerable problems. There must be ways of overcoming the problems and improving the economies of scale.

↓ *Figure 10.2:*
The Leadenhall Building, London

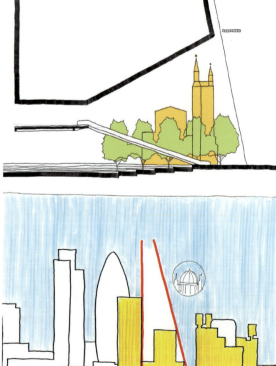

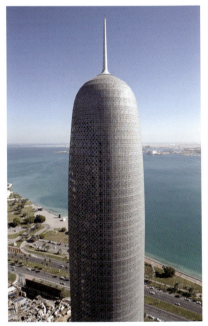

In the case of rain, many sustainability rating systems, such as LEED, now award points for rainwater capture and recycling, but in the case of most tall buildings the area of capture is usually a part of the tower or podium roof. In the context of skyscraper forms, however, the roof is a negligible area in comparison to the façade, especially when one considers that rain at height does not fall vertically but is typically driven in a horizontal plane by wind. Thus perhaps the true potential of rainwater capture is in the façade and this could become an influence on some tall buildings.

3. Tall buildings should relate to the cultural characteristics of place

The cultural aspects of place are less tangible and therefore harder to define. Culture is more connected with the patterns of life in a city and how this manifests itself in the customs, activities and expressions of the people. Culture can thus be embraced in a literal way in the building, as demonstrated by the 1984 Dayabumi Complex in Kuala Lumpur, with its Islamic outer façade skin an interpretation of the vernacular *jali* screen (though this also has the significant added benefit of shielding the curtain wall behind from direct solar gain – see Figure 10.4). As seen in Figure 10.5, this concept was modified on the Doha Tower in 2012.

↖ *Figure 10.3:*
Pearl River Tower, Guangzhou

↑↑ *Figure 10.4:*
Dayabumi Complex, Kuala Lumpur

↑ *Figure 10.5:*
Doha Tower, Qatar

↑ *Figure 10.6:*
Burj Khalifa,
Dubai

4. Variation with height in form, texture and function Tall buildings should not
be monolithic vertical extrusions of an efficient floor plan, but should vary in form, use and expression
with height. This variance in form should be inspired by the city, both physically and environmentally.

The great heights being achieved with tall buildings today effectively means that we are designing
single tall buildings that cut across multiple climate zones. The external air temperature at the Burj
Khalifa in Dubai (see Figure 10.6), for example, is reported to be 8–10°C cooler at the top of the
building than at the bottom, so this could be reflected in the form, façade, systems and even use mix of
the building. A tall building should thus be considered as a number of stacked communities according
to the opportunities of each specific 'horizon', both climatically and physically in its relation to the city.

This could manifest itself in the manipulation of building mass as well as function, and there should
also be variance in skin and texture throughout the building, depending on the responsibilities of
each different horizon within the form. The MEP and other systems would also vary (at the very least
air intake should occur at the top of the tower, to take advantage of several degrees of free cooling).

5. Maximise layers of usage for all systems and materials Traditional
constituents of tall buildings need to be challenged to increase the usefulness of the typology in
sustainable cities of the future. This should occur on two levels:

(i) the type of functions that are traditionally accommodated within tall buildings, and

(ii) the number of functions that are accommodated in a single tall building.

Tall buildings have the versatility to accommodate uses other than the standard office, residential
and hotel functions that currently predominate. A mix of uses gives opportunity for more duality, for
aspects such as waste heat generated through one function being used in another, for car parking/
sharing, for supporting functions and servicing. Such mutual interdependence and variation is
achieved in a few outstanding examples, such as the Abeno Harukas building in Osaka, Japan, which
adds schools, a museum and a medical clinic to the typical mix.

The BioSkin system on the 2011 NBF Osaki building in Tokyo (see Figure 10.7), operates a sun-
shading system that not only shields the interior spaces from solar gain but contains recycled
rainwater that evaporates through the ceramic skin when heated by the sun, simultaneously lowering
the urban heat island effect.

6. Tall buildings should provide significant, communal, open recreational space

More open, communal, recreational spaces need to be introduced into tall buildings. This means breaking away from the perception of maximum financial return on every square metre of floor space. Such spaces have been proven to improve the quality of the internal environment, which has a direct impact on saleable/rental return, satisfaction of occupants and productivity of workers. In addition, the inclusion of these spaces can enable a sense of community to develop. Social sustainability on an urban scale is a major challenge for our future cities.

The 1997 Commerzbank, Frankfurt (see Figure 10.8), despite being almost two decades old, is still one of the most significant tall buildings with sky gardens; every occupant has direct physical access to one of the ten four-storey sky gardens spiralling up the building (which are also part of its natural ventilation strategy). This commercial building could also serve as an excellent model for an idealised residential building, with narrow, cross-ventilated floors of residential apartments grouped around a 'garden in the sky' where a sense of community can develop.

Even taller and more recent buildings have offered variations on this, such as the Bow in Calgary (2012), which features several intermediate sky lobbies with atria, and Shanghai Tower (2015), which wraps a twisting double skin around nine stacked zones, each with a 14-storey sky garden.

↑ *Figure 10.7:*
NBF Osaki building, Tokyo (left), featuring BioSkin (right)

↓ *Figure 10.8:*
Commerzbank, Frankfurt

↓ *Figure 10.9:*
014, Dubai

↓↓ *Figure 10.10:*
One Central Park,
Sydney

7. Introduce more façade envelope opacity Tall buildings should be designed with more envelope opacity from the outset. This approach is in contrast to an all-glass transparent skin requiring significant external shading devices to control the light, heat and glare. Although the impacts on both internal daylighting and views out need to be balanced, all-glass towers do not make sense, especially in intensely hot solar environments. In addition, greater façade opacity gives an opportunity for greater thermal mass to allow the envelope to be more insulated from external temperature and climate variations. This also gives the opportunity for wider façade variance and expression, as evidenced by projects such as 014 in Dubai (see Figure 10.9), the National Commerce Bank in Jeddah, Saudi Arabia, and the aforementioned Doha Tower in Qatar.

8. Embrace organic vegetation In those climates that allow, vegetation should become an essential part of the external and internal material palette for tall buildings. The benefits of vegetation on both the building and urban scale are now better understood [Wood, Bahrami and Safarik, 2014]. The approach can offer increased shading and thermal insulation of the building envelope, improved air quality (both internally and externally), reduction of urban heat island effect, carbon sequestering, oxygen generation, sound absorption, possible agricultural produce, provision of natural habitat for insects and small animals, as well as the psychological benefits for both building and urban dwellers. Great things are now being achieved with greenery in tall buildings, particularly in Singapore, but also in other cities globally, as evidenced by the 2014 One Central Park building in Sydney (see Figure 10.10). In the context of this chapter, the adoption of local vegetation (which is already hardy to the environment) would also contribute to the localised aesthetic of the building, since even if every tall building the world over were cloaked in greenery, they would all reflect their local indigenous plant species in the same way that the fields and forests of every region around the world are different.

9. Introduce physical, circulatory and programmatic connections between tall buildings: skybridges It is counterintuitive that as cities are making a push for ever-denser, ever-taller urban form, they allow only the ground plane to be the physical means of connection between towers. Skybridges have the potential to enrich both tall buildings and cities, allow the sharing of resources between towers (spatial as well as service infrastructure), improve evacuation options, and reduce energy consumption through allowing horizontal as well as vertical movement between towers. In Hong Kong and many other cities in China, we often see numerous identical residential towers side by side in long rows – five, six, seven towers – often separated by just a few metres, but with vacant fire refuge floors all lined up at the same level. What leap of imagination would it take to physically connect these vacant refuge floors with skybridges, simultaneously giving more fire evacuation routes and creating the potential for communal zones in the sky? Some building designers and owners are now recognising this, with projects such as Singapore's 2009 Pinnacle@Duxton housing scheme connecting seven residential towers with skybridges and skyparks at two levels, containing gardens, jogging tracks and significant urban habitat (see Figure 10.11). Elsewhere in Singapore, the 2010 Marina Bay Sands Hotel placed a massive swimming pool atop a skybridge connecting three towers.

10. We need to bring ALL aspects of the city up into the sky

If cities embrace the principle that the dense vertical city is more sustainable than the dispersed horizontal city, then we need to recognise that the ground level is an essential support layer to the people who live in cities now, where the essential elements of life in the city are largely contained: circulation, recreation, education, shopping, health and, most crucially, where a sense of community forms. Thus, if we are looking to concentrate perhaps 100 times more people on the same quantity of land through building tall, then we need to replicate these facilities that exist at the ground plane up in the sky, including the parks and the sidewalks, the schools and clinics, the shops and sports facilities, and many other public and civic functions. The ground plane thus needs to be considered as an essential

↓ *Figure 10.11:*
Pinnacle@Duxton,
Singapore

Consider a low-rise urban scenario
Current population: 1 million

Ground plane = All urban "infrastructure": physical, spatial, circulation, recreational, communal, etc.

Population growth & urbanisation: Driving the 1 million to 10 million inhabitants: where do they go?

Horizontal growth of the city = Unsustainable

Population growth & urbanisation: Vertical growth = Concentrated land & resource use. More sustainable?

Overburden of the ground plan / infrastructure, and disconnected icons?

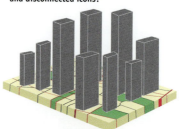

This is not a sustainable way forward

The tall building as a piece of the city flipped vertically...

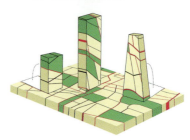

... including the infrastructure

Replication of the ground plane & connectivity of infrastructure

Towards Sustainable Vertical Urbanism...

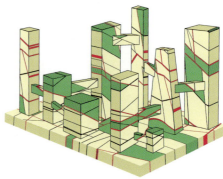

↑ → *Figure 10.12: A vision for a vertical city*

↓ *Figure 10.13: the Interlace, Singapore, 2014*

layer of the city that needs to be at least partially replicated at strategic horizons within and between buildings in the sky; not in place of the ground plane, but in support of it (see Figure 10.12).

A look at a visionary project like the Interlace, completed in 2014 in Singapore (see Figure 10.13), gives some indication of how the 'tower in the park' model could be advanced. Here there are numerous ground planes all over the project, and the skewed floor plans of the rectilinear basic forms stacked atop one another create an almost infinite sense of variety, while offering streets, parks and communal life at various heights and scales.

A Vision of the Future?

There is a growing consciousness of the tremendous amounts of energy tall buildings consume, not only in daily operations but in their entire lifecycle, from sourcing raw materials to a subject rarely considered when a building is being conceived – its demolition. Meanwhile, the requirements to reduce cost, maximise profit and accelerate construction while upholding high standards of quality and safety have never been more demanding.

Recently, attention has turned towards new materials and methods for assembling, operating and disassembling tall buildings. Two trends once on the outer periphery of thought are now being slowly integrated into practice, though much more remains to be done.

J57, a 57-storey building in Changsha, China was constructed in 2015 at the rate of three floors per day using prefabricated modules (for further discussion of this practice, see Chapter 8, pp. 120-121). Of course, this and its predecessors were undertaken under ideal conditions on company-controlled worksites well outside populated areas. In tighter, messier environments like New York and London, prefab has proven problematic, as the entire supply chain of materials, labour and transport that creates tall buildings today had to be rethought for a pioneering project. So far, the promised savings and efficiencies have proven elusive, except where skilled labour is extremely hard to procure.

Interestingly, one of the most exciting future materials for tall building construction is one of the oldest – wood (see also Chapter 5, pp. 81-82). The idea of a 40- or 50-storey skyscraper made of wood is anathema to those familiar with 'stick-built' balloon-framing commonly used on one-to-five-storey buildings. But new products, such as cross-laminated timber (CLT) – essentially a composite of members glued together to form shear walls with the fire resistance and bearing strengths of steel and concrete – are changing mindsets. The recyclability and renewability of wood turns buildings into carbon sequestration sinks, rather than landfill fodder. Of course, fire codes are heavily biased against wood structures, as they are based on the prevailing framing techniques used today. 'Woodscrapers', then, may be a uniquely regional condition for some time to come, popping up in places like Sweden, Finland and British Columbia, which have much to gain (and a local-sourcing argument to make) from a revived market for wood.

For the high-rise office world to adapt new technologies, it will have to be shown that new approaches will not only improve the general constructability of tall buildings but will also enhance and support the dynamic occupancy trends that are covered elsewhere in this book.

How will this happen? The principles outlined above are reflective of a utopian ideal, and considerable technical, operational and financial challenges exist around their realisation. Currently, in most cities the responsibility for urban infrastructure – pavements, roads, parks, power, lighting, waste, sewage, etc. – lies with the local government, but its involvement in the built environment stops at the front door of buildings. The building itself becomes the responsibility of the developer alone, especially financially, with the local government only providing oversight. But achieving what is suggested above involves the creation of an urban, public infrastructure inside the buildings, and thus we need to rethink how our buildings are financed and realised. Each building needs to become a public–private partnership, with the spatial and public infrastructure in the building being financed by the local government, the same as it would be in the low-rise horizontal realm. And to deliver this, an overall three-dimensional, long-term, stratified-in-height plan would need to be created.

Which brings us back to one of the main challenges for the typology into the future: how can we create tall buildings that are relevant to the specifics of place – physically, environmentally and culturally? We need tall buildings that maximise their connection to the city, climate and people. The future of our cities, and perhaps our continued survival on this planet, relies on it.

Afterword

Tall buildings have much greater permanence than their low-rise counterparts. The changes to a skyline that such buildings create can be strong symbols of growth and a dynamic city, but where tall buildings are poorly positioned or lacking in quality, impacts can be negative and equally long lasting. They will impact the skyline for many years to come, perhaps arguably forever, so their quality and context is fundamental to their success and acceptance.

There is little doubt that the quality of our tall buildings has increased over time, but even more important is the realisation that their contribution to the urban landscape and the public realm is what really makes a tall building successful. The creation of public space, both around and within our tall buildings, allows everyone to enjoy them – not just the select few who work or live within them. Many of the buildings which have been chosen to illustrate this book are testament to this.

The preceding chapters have shown that thinking and caring about the scale and impact of high rise is critical from the very earliest stages of a project. The care and attention from the many stakeholders who give permission, fund, design, construct and occupy tall buildings, and absorb them into the community, is crucial to creating a successful high rise. In addition, we hope to have given a glimpse into the complexity, ingenuity and magnitude of the detail necessary to realise the product.

Creating a building is never an easy task and setting the building in context is always a challenge. Delivering tall buildings has become more complex over time, requiring a wide range of expertise within a strict framework. With the current economic pressures, the drive for efficiency and reduced construction costs requires innovation and challenges previous standards. New materials and construction techniques are continually being devised, allowing faster, safer and more cost effective tall buildings in the future.

In the 2002 book, *Cradle to Cradle*, by William McDonough and Michael Braungart, the authors argue that products should be designed for continuous renewal or should avoid being down cycled into low grade use. This second edition of *Tall Buildings* considers a variety of visions of the future where we recognise the longevity of the building and imagine future use, thus recycling to retain value. The evolution of high rise is a continuous process of adaptation, comparable to natural world responses to environmental, socioeconomic and commercial constraints.

The need and desire for tall buildings in order to cope with the densification of our cities, and the human desire to build taller and taller, will continue over time. The accolade of being the tallest building in the world still captures our imagination and will drive us higher and higher well into the future.

All these considerations drove the structure for this new edition, as well as the desire to cover such a wide range of intertwined subjects, all of which are fundamental to the creation of successful tall buildings for the enjoyment of everyone. If this publication helps in some small way to deliver one single better tall building through the knowledge shared by the contributors, then the effort will have been worthwhile.

Nigel Clark and Bill Price

Bibliography

Documents and publications

BCO Guide to Specification for Offices 2014

BCO/Savills report, 'What Workers Want', 2013

CTBUH, *Tall Buildings Reference Book*, 2013

Johnson, Boris, Mayor of London, '2020 Vision: The Greatest City on Earth, Ambitions for London', Greater London Authority, 2013

Joornweg, Daniel and Kevin Pope, 'Socioeconomic Pathways and Regional Distribution of the World's 101 Largest Cities', Global Cities Institute Working Paper No. 4, January 2014

Kayashima, Y. Shinozaki, T. Koga and H. Ichihara, 'A New Demolition System for High-Rise Buildings', Asia Ascending CTBUH 9th World Congress Shanghai 2012 Proceedings, pp. 631-36

Knight Frank report, 'Skyscrapers', 2015

Mizutani, R. and S. Yoshikai, 'A New Demolition Method for Tall Buildings, Kajima Cut & Take Down Method', *CTBUH Journal* (4), pp. 36-41

New London Architecture and GL Hearn, London Tall Buildings Survey, March 2015

Murray, Peter, *The Saga of Sydney Opera House*, Routledge, 2003

Trabucco, Dario and Paolo Fava, 'Confronting the Question of Demolition or Renovation', *CTBUH Journal*, 2013, Issue IV, pp. 38-43

Willis, Carol, *Form Follows Finance*, Princeton University Press, 1995, p. 217

Wood, Antony, Payam, Bahrami, and Daniel Safarik, *Green Walls in High-Rise Buildings: An output of the CTBUH Sustainability Working Group,* Images Publishing, 2014.

Websites

http://vincent.callebaut.org/page1-img-asiancairns.html

http://www.theguardian.com/world/2015/apr/30/chinese-construction-firm-erects-57-storey-skyscraper-in-19-days

http://www.waughthistleton.com/project.php?name=murray

http://www.creebyrhomberg.com/en/projects/

Adamson Associates *63*

AbI flexible space *78 (top)*

Jahangir Ahmed *14*

alinea *100, 101*

Aon UK Ltd *53*

ARC Studio Architecture + Urbanism/Singapore Housing & Development Board *139*

Ateliers Jean Nouvel/photo CSCEC *135 (bottom right)*

Meike Borchers, WSP | Parsons Brinckerhoff *82*

Filip Bramorski/CC BY-SA 2.0/Wikimedia Commons [1] *132-33 (top)*

Principal Tower is a joint development by Brookfield Property Partners L.P., Concord Pacific and W1 Developments *12-13*

Richard Bryant, courtesy of British Land/ Oxford Properties *134 (bottom left)*

Canary Wharf Group plc *11 (bottom), 17 (right), 107 (right)*

Canary Wharf Group plc; photographer: Peter Matthews *32*

Canary Wharf Group plc; photographer: Philip Vile *106-07*

CapitaLand, photograph by Iwan Baan *130, 140 (bottom)*

Cazz/CC BY 2.0 UK/Flickr [2] *132-33 (middle bottom)*

Samantha-Jay Clegg *11 (top)*

Council on Tall Buildings and Urban Habitat (CTBUH) *2-5, 127 (top), 140 (top)*

J. Crocker/CC BY-SA 3.0/Wikimedia Commons [3] *25*

DBOX, courtesy Eric Parry Architects *6, 43*

Despe *122*

Nicola Evans, WSP | Parsons Brinckerhoff *iv (bottom), 0, 10, 16, 59, 66, 70 (bottom), 80, 89, 98, 108, 111 (top right), 112 (top), 113, 114, 116, 117*

Farrells *30, 33-34, 45-47*

Michael Ficeto, The Hearst Corporation *81*

Gensler *9 (top), 50, 52, 54 (bottom left and right), 55 (top and bottom left), 56*

Marshal Gerometta/CTBUH *125, 126 (top)*

Greater London Authority *38 (top left), 39 (top right), 40*

Mike Gonzalez *132-33 (bottom)*

Aurelien Guichard/CC BY-SA 2.0/Wikimedia Commons [1] *15*

Steven Henry *126 (bottom)*

Herzog & de Meuron *17 (left), 48*

Hilson Moran *iv (top), 76-77, 78 (bottom), 79 (top), 83-85, 87 (right), 90, 96, 97*

Nick Hufton, Hufton + Crow Photography *54 (top), 79 (bottom)*

Jeddah Economic Company/Adrian Smith + Gordon Gill Architecture *74-75*

Kajima Corporation *129 (bottom)*

Kloniwotski/CC BY-SA 2.0/Flickr [1] *9 (bottom)*

Laing O'Rourke *110, 111 (top left and bottom), 115, 120*

Lipton Rogers *72 (right)*

Markel International; photographer Matthew Joseph *24, 26, 28-29*

William Moore, Deutsche Bank *127 (bottom), 128*

Tansri Muliani *135 (left)*

Ian Muttoo/CC BY-SA 2.0/Wikimedia Commons [1] *44*

Mylius/CC BY-SA 3.0/Wikimedia Commons [3] *42*

Mstyslav-Chernov/CC-BY-SA-3.0/Wikimedia Commons [3] *20*

Olegmj-Dreamstime.com *136 (right)*

John Parker, WSP | Parsons Brinckerhoff *112 (bottom)*

Yogesh Patil, Greater London Authority *38-39 (bottom)*

Pelli Clarke Pelli Architects *87 (left)*

Roberto Portolese *138 (bottom)*

Andrew Pratt, WSP | Parsons Brinckerhoff *93, 94*

Darren Pullen, WSP | Parsons Brinckerhoff *119*

Reiser+Umemoto, RUR Architecture *129 (top)*

Rhubarb *55 (bottom right)*

Gabriel Rodriguez/CC BY-SA 2.0/Wikimedia Commons [1] *34-35*

Rogers Stirk Harbour + Partners *134 (top and bottom right)*

Nikken Sekkei *137 (top)*

Shanghai Tower Business Operation and Management Co. Ltd. *18, 22, 27*

SHoP Architects *60-61, 71*

Image courtesy of Skanska *121*

Ron Slade, WSP |Parsons Brinckerhoff *69 (top)*

Taisei Corporation *129 (top)*

Dario Trabucco *124*

Matt H. Wade/CC BY-SA 3.0/Wikimedia Commons [3] *132-33 (middle top)*

Peter Weismantle *136 (left)*

Colin Wilson, Greater London Authority *36*

Dr Antony Wood *135 (top right)*

WSP | Parsons Brinckerhoff *58, 68, 69 (bottom), 70 (top and middle), 72 (left), 73, 88*

Nigel Young – Foster + Partners *137 (bottom)*

[1] https://creativecommons.org/licenses/by-sa/2.0/

[2] https://creativecommons.org/licenses/by/2.0/

[3] https://creativecommons.org/licenses/by-sa/3.0/deed.en

Index